W9-BKB-783

FROMMER'S

BED AND BREAKFAST GUIDES

MID-ATLANTIC

NEW YORK, NEW JERSEY, PENNSYLVANIA, MARYLAND, VIRGINIA, WASHINGTON, D.C.

By HAL GIESEKING, W. LYNN SELDON Jr., NAOMI BLACK,
GALE ZUCKER, TERRY BERGER, and ROBERTA GARDNER

Photographs by Hal Gieseking, W. Lynn Seldon Jr.,
Gale Zucker, and George W. Gardner

DESIGNED AND PRODUCED BY
ROBERT R. REID AND TERRY BERGER

MACMILLAN • USA

Frontispiece: detail at the Vandiver Inn, Havre de Grace, Maryland.

The front cover photograph and the
 photographs of 1880 House on Long Island
on pages 26 and 27 and those of the Inn at
Centre Park in Reading on pages 66 and 67
were taken by Giammarino and Dworkin.

Published by Macmillan Travel
A Prentice Hall Macmillan Company
15 Columbus Circle
New York, NY 10023

MACMILLAN is a registered trademark of Macmillian, Inc.

Library of Congress Card No. 1085-9802
ISBN 0-02-860880-1

A Robert Reid Associates production
Typeset in Bodoni Book by Monotype Composition Company, Baltimore
Produced by Mandarin Offset, Hong Kong
Printed in Hong Kong

1 2 3 4 5 6 7 8 9 10

MID-ATLANTIC

*The rising sun calls guests to breakfast
at the Vandiver Inn, Havre de Grace, Maryland.*

CONTENTS

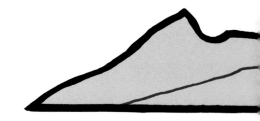

NEW YORK

DAVE MONAGHAN PHOTOGRAPH

PLUMBUSH

A jewel

Surrounded by a grove of towering maple trees and bedecked in mauve and pale pink with soft green and teal trim, Plumbush has been thoughtfully restored to its former Victorian elegance. Sandy Green first noticed the house as she rode to school on the bus. After growing up and moving out West, she and her husband George have returned to Chautauqua County and established a jewel of a bed and breakfast.

Each of the four bedchambers is named after a species of plum: Pipestone, the largest of the rooms; Bluefre, bedecked in blues and pinks; Greengage, a smaller accommodation, and the Bradshaw, a guest room with twin beds. Each is decorated in a unique blend of Victorian and country antiques with well-crafted reproductions. Some have armoires and wicker furniture. Nothing has escaped the innkeeper's eye. Even the nightstand drawers are filled with curiosities like fragrant sachets, a Victorian valentine, a postcard, a book of poetry, old spectacles, or a weathered copy of *The Farmer's Almanac*.

Chocolate-chip muffins or Sandy's peach coffee cake often highlight the generous continental breakfast eaten in the dining room or on the enclosed porch. Through the tall arched windows you can look out over small garden areas, and across acres of fields and woodlands.

Ninety miles from Niagara Falls, and just twelve miles from Lake Erie, Plumbush is less than a mile from the world-famous Chautauqua Institution, to whose lectures, study groups, opera, dance, and numerous musical events people flock every summer.

PLUMBUSH, Chautauqua-Stedman Road, Box 332, RD 2, Mayville, NY 14757; (716) 789-5309; Sandy and George Green, owners. Open all year. Five guest rooms with private baths. Rates: $85 to $100 double, including expanded continental breakfast. Children 12 and over welcome; no pets; smoking outside only; Visa/MasterCard/Discover. Recommended dining at The Curly Maple, Webb's. Cross-country and downhill skiing and snowmobiling in winter. Golf, sailing, in summer. Great antiquing and birding.

DIRECTIONS: from Rte. 17 take exit 7 onto Rte. 33 north for 3 miles.

ROSEWOOD INN

Unique character and charm

This 1,855 Greek Revival mansion was transformed into an English Tudor in 1917 and is now a bed and breakfast, presided over by popular local newspaper editor Dick Peer, and his wife, Winnie. It is a first-class hostelry in the finest tradition.

Six guest rooms, named after popular figures, offer their own unique character and charm. The Jenny Lind Room features sheet music and programs from the Swedish Nightingale's concerts; the Herman Melville Room, Gloucester whaling prints and a harpoon on the mantel; the Charles Dana Gibson Room, Gibson Girl prints and Eastlake furniture.

The Corning Glass Museum, within walking distance of Rosewood Inn, houses the most extensive glass collection in the world. On display are ancient Egyptian, Roman, Venetian, and Persian glass, and a vast Tiffany window of a scene overlooking the Hudson.

The Rockwell Museum, also nearby, features the largest collection of Western art in the eastern United States.

ROSEWOOD INN, 134 East First St., Corning, NY 14830; (607) 962-3253; Suzanne and Stewart Sanders, owners. Open all year. Seven guest rooms, all with private baths and air conditioning. Rates $80 to 125, including full breakfast. Children welcome over 12; no pets; no smoking on premises; Visa/MasterCard/Diners Club/American Express. Scenic Finger Lakes, Watkins Glen, auto racing, wineries, Ithaca and its universities within a short drive.

DIRECTIONS: take Rte. 17 through downtown Corning. East First Street parallels Rte. 17 one block to the south.

The Jenny Lind Room.

PHOTOGRAPHS COURTESY ROSEWOOD INN

STAGECOACH INN

Its own brand of romance

Bustling Lake Placid Village lies tucked between two shimmering bodies of water. Shallow and tranquil Mirror Lake laps up to the town's center. Just a few miles north, Lake Placid serves as the village's reservoir, reaching spring-fed depths of over 300 feet—an angler's paradise with native fish as well as upwards of 10,000 rainbow and lake trout stocked by the state each year.

Sports activities are a large part of village life. Many of the 1980 Winter Olympic structures continue to bring in world-class championships throughout the year.

The 1833 clapboard Stagecoach Inn sits two miles northwest of the ski jumps on a back street away from traffic and village noise. Rustic and casual, the inn delivers its own brand of romance to its guests. Warmed by a fireplace, the two-story cathedral-ceilinged living room invites sitting back and enjoying the Adirondack-style details that once marked an era of extravagant parties and stimulating conversation. Yellow birch logs and twigs form the mantel, bookshelves, and support beams, as well as an imposing banister that leads to a second floor balcony.

The view down to the living room makes a still life *extraordinaire*. A deer head rests comfortably above the fireplace, a working Mason and Hamlin organ stands to the left, and on the side wall crossed snowshoes hang over framed photos of former innkeepers Mr. and Mrs. Lyons.

The other common area, the dining room, encloses its visitors with Georgia pine on the walls, ceiling, and floors. A cozy fire reflects in the wood's sheen, casting an amber radiance on the morning meal—a perfect touch to start any day.

THE STAGECOACH INN, Old Military Road, Lake Placid, NY 12946: (518) 523-9474; Peter Moreau, inn owner; Lyn Witte, innkeeper. Open all year. Nine cozy guest rooms, five with private baths, two with fireplaces. Rates: $55 to $85, single; $60 to $85, double: $10 for an additional person. Children over 6 welcome; inquire about pets. Sports activities nearby include golf, hiking, rock climbing, trout fishing, horseback riding. Skating school ice shows every Saturday night in session; stadium jumping horse show in early summer.

DIRECTIONS: from the Adirondack Northway (Rte. 87), take Rte. 73N for 30 miles. Bear left just past the ski jumps (where the Saranac Lake sign is pointing). The inn is about two miles down on the left.

MT. TREMPER INN

A sprawling country mansion

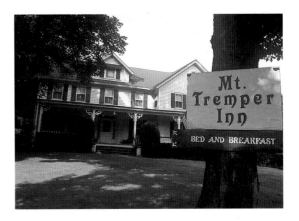

At first glance the Mt. Tremper Inn looks like a sprawling country mansion, which is exactly what it was when built in 1850. Step inside and you'll find a veritable museum of nineteenth-century antiques. In the parlor you'll discover a Louis XVI chair circa 1840, ladies chairs from the Renaissance Revival circa 1860, and even a wind-up 1892 Regina box that still plays the *Blue Danube Waltz.*

But this is no "don't touch" museum. Guests can lounge on the period furniture before a blue fieldstone fireplace as they plan their skiing activities in the winter (Hunter Mountain and Bellaire Mountain ski areas are only 16 miles away). Summer visitors can tube and swim down the Esopus Creek and shop among the boutiques of Woodstock just ten miles away.

Guest rooms are named for little hamlets in the area: Shandaken, Chichester, Woodstock. The Wittenberg Suite, generously proportioned at eighteen by twenty-eight feet, was formerly a parlor.

A buffet breakfast is available each day that includes Mt. Tremper's homemade granola and a tasty baked egg dish. Guests are free to dine on the veranda or in the large breakfast room, possibly to the distant strains of the *Blue Danube.*

MT. TREMPER INN. corner of Rte. 212 and Wittenberg Road; mail: P.O. Box 51, Mt. Tremper, NY 12457; (914) 688-5329; Lou Caselli and Peter LaScala, hosts. Open all year. Twelve guest rooms, two with private baths. Each of the other guest rooms has a sink and shares hallway baths. Rates: $68 to $98 per room, including a full buffet breakfast. No children or pets; no smoking; Visa/MasterCard.

DIRECTIONS: I-87 to Kingston, then Rte. 28 to the intersection with Rte. 212; turn right on Rte. 212 for ⅓ mile to first intersection.

The colorful guest lounge.

The massive front of the main building.

THE MERRILL MAGEE HOUSE

Growing since 1839

In 1839 Stephen Griffin II purchased some land in Warrensburg, New York, that came with a tiny house. Following the fashion of the time, he added a tall-columned Greek Revival front. In later years new owners moved an 1812 building from a nearby homestead and joined it to the back of the house, and built a private swimming pool (said to be the oldest private pool in New York State). This elongated building became a well-known inn, serving breakfasts and dinners seven days a week.

The present innkeepers, Ken and Florence Carrington, must have caught the building bug from previous owners because they built the Peletiah Richards Guest House (designed by their son, an architect) right behind the main inn.

The main inn has a two bedroom suite that is perfect for families and can accommodate up to five people. Stephen Griffin himself would probably still feel right at home in these rooms, with their old-fashioned wallpaper, country quilts, and a claw foot tub.

The contemporary guest house offers ten rooms,

Left below, the oldest private swimming pool in New York.

Breakfast is served at separate tables.

nine with queen or king beds and one with twin beds. Each of these rooms has a private bath and a working fireplace. This is the perfect place to begin exploring the Adirondacks (hiking, skiing, boating) and nearby Lake George.

THE MERRILL MAGEE HOUSE. 2 Hudson St., Warrensburg, NY 12425; (518) 623-2449; Ken and Florence Carrington, hosts. Open all year. Seven guest rooms in the Peletiah Richards Guest House, one family suite in the main inn. Rates: $75 to $95 single, $105 to $125 double in the guest house; $150 for the family suite, including full breakfasts served to individual tables. Children welcome in family suite only; no pets; smoking is limited (ask host); all major credit cards.

DIRECTIONS: take Adirondack Northway (I-87) to exit 23, follow sign to Warrensburg.

The grand stairway in the guest house.

A light and cheerful guest room.

THE INN ON BEACON HILL

Off to the races

Saratoga Springs is a resort city with a languid Victorian past and fast-paced entertainments such as thoroughbred horse racing and regular performances by many of the world's top singers, dancers, and musicians. But one thing hasn't changed. Just as celebrities came for "the waters" at the turn of the century, travelers still soak in the famous hot mineral baths.

Only a few miles away, The Inn on Beacon Hill offers a rural retreat for anyone who wants to sample all the pleasures of Saratoga Springs, then come home at night to a peaceful farmhouse flanked by a gazebo, flower gardens, and acres of farmland as far as the eye can see. Innkeeper Andrea Collins-Breslin greets guests in her Victorian parlor and introduces them to their rooms. For example, there is the Tulip Room with its four-poster queen bed, the Queen Anne's Lace Room with a spindle queen bed, or the Victorian Parlor Suite with a two-poster queen bed and its own parlor with a baby grand piano. Andrea

Left, innkeeper Andrea Collins-Breslin.

THE INN ON BEACON HILL, P.O. Box 1462, Saratoga Springs, NY 12866; (518) 695-3693; Andrea Collins-Breslin, innkeeper. Open all year. Four air conditioned rooms, including a Parlor Suite. Two of the rooms have private baths, one bath is shared by two rooms. Rates: $65 to $85; during the thoroughbred racing season (mid-July to August) rates rise to $115 to $125; includes full breakfast. Children over 12 welcome; no pets; smoking only on porch and grounds; Visa/MasterCard.
DIRECTIONS: call.

then enjoys telling guests about the "fabulous antiquing," the Saratoga National Historic Park, the New York City Ballet in July, the Philadelphia Orchestra in August, and the thoroughbred racing from July to late August. And much, much more.

But she also wants guests to save time to sit in her gazebo, walk the gardens, and enjoy the full country breakfast she serves each morning in her large dining room.

The guest parlor.

A guest room.

SARATOGA ROSE INN

Gourmet breakfasts

The Saratoga Rose, just 16 miles from the bustling resort towns of Lake George and Saratoga Springs, offers a romantic, turn-of-the-century respite in the rugged beauty of the Adirondack Mountains.

The late Queen Anne-Victorian, cheerfully trimmed in purple and rose hues, was built in 1885 as a gift to a bride. The skill of the original Adirondack artisans who built it is evident throughout the mansion, with its intricately inlaid and parquet wood floors, forty stained-glass windows, and an amazing terra-cotta corner fireplace in the entryway.

A lot of love—literally—went into the restoration of the home in 1988, when newlyweds Tony and Nancy Merlino bought and renovated it as part of their honeymoon. Two months later, guests began to arrive, and have been basking in their hospitality ever since.

The Merlinos were able to preserve or match much of the original wallpaper and filled the Saratoga Rose with romantic country Victoriana. Upstairs, five period guest rooms offer privacy and comfort. The spacious, blue Queen Anne Room is popular with newlyweds and honeymooners, with its wood-and-tile fireplace and quilt-covered bed.

Guests staying in the Garden Room may think they have found a little piece of heaven. Decorated in shades of green and cream, with a carved spindle bed, the room has French doors that open on to a private balcony with a Jacuzzi. Highly recommended after a day spent exploring the area is a mug of Tony's liqueur-laced Adirondack coffee from the bar downstairs, and a soak under the stars in the Jacuzzi.

Guests wishing for fine dining need look no further than downstairs, where Chef Anthony Merlino presides over a first-class restaurant. Guests may have dinner served in their room, or reserve a table in the romantic wood-trimmed dining room.

Breakfast specialties include perfectly done Grand Marnier French toast, with maple syrup tapped from a tree on the property. Another offering, eggs Anthony, was so appreciated by a guest that she dubbed it Eggs *Saint* Anthony!

SARATOGA ROSE INN & RESTAURANT, P.O. Box 238, Hadley, NY 12835; (800) 942-5025, (518) 696-2861, Fax (518) 696-5319; Anthony and Nancy Merlino, owners. Open all year. Five guest rooms with private baths and one with working fireplace and one with private balcony and Jacuzzi. Rates: $85 to $165, including full breakfast in room or in dining room. Well behaved children over 12 welcome; no pets; no smoking in guest rooms; major credit cards accepted. All activities available locally.

DIRECTIONS: available on reservation.

Innkeepers Anthony and Nancy Merlino.

THE LAMPLIGHT INN

Romance in the Adirondacks

There is a room diary in each guest room of the Lamplight Inn. Over the years many of the occupants have recorded their innermost thoughts while staying in the room, about the rekindling of romances and the joyful celebration of weddings and anniversaries.

The subject of all the guests' praise is a Victorian Gothic building constructed for a wealthy bachelor in 1890 as a summer residence. He loved to entertain in style, hence the huge Great Room with twelve-foot-high beamed ceilings and chestnut wainscoting.

When Gene and Linda Merlino purchased this aging structure in 1984, they immediately thought of its bed and breakfast possibilities. The home retains much of its early charm, with many comfortable and attractive new touches added by Linda and Gene. Each of the ten guest rooms has its own personality; six have gas-burning fireplaces, all are centrally air conditioned, and all have romantic ceiling fans. The Skylight Room lives up to its name with a cathedral ceiling sloping up to a skylight. The Rose Room is extra large (the home's original master bedroom) with a draped black iron canopy bed.

Near Lake George and Saratoga Springs, the area abounds with winter and summer activities. These include swimming at the beach on Lake Luzerne (about a minute from the house), white water rafting, a winter carnival, and special concerts at the Luzerne Music Center. Much to write home about—or in the room diary at bedside.

THE LAMPLIGHT INN. 2129 Lake Avenue; mail: P.O. Box 70, Lake Luzerne, NY 12846; 1-800-BNB-INNV for reservations or (518) 696-5294 for information; Gene and Linda Merlino, hosts/owners. Open all year (except for Christmas Eve and Christmas Day). Ten guest rooms, all with queen beds and private baths. Rates (changing seasonally): $85 to $150, including huge breakfasts served at individual tables. Children over 12 welcome; no pets; No smoking in bedrooms or dining room; all major credit cards.

DIRECTIONS: take Adirondack Northway (I-87) to Lake Luzerne exit. The Inn is located on Rte. 9N in the center of Lake Luzerne.

The parlor with period furnishings.

THE J. P. SILL HOUSE

An elegant showcase of wallpapers

Formal elegance betrays a studied warmth in the J.P. Sill House, a showcase of impeccably designed and printed wallpapers. The handscreened "room sets" may include as many as seven different yet harmonious patterns. All are based on original works by turn-of-the-century artists. A previous innkeeper discovered the California firm of Bradbury & Bradbury from a newspaper article; an inquiry and a visit to the firm convinced her to paper the house with these carefully chosen designs. The results are spectacular.

The green-hued formal dining room carries an Eastlake frieze paper initially reproduced for the Cameron-Stanford House in Oakland, California; the fill paper, a graceful willow pattern, is attributed to William Morris. Both become richer when sunlight filters in through the room's French doors that open

Left above, the elaborately decorated sitting room is a good example of the inspired use of wallpaper. Below, one of the guest rooms.

onto one of the inn's porches.

Beautiful fabrics successfully interplay and blend with the wallpapers—Schumacher, Greeff, and Scalamandre silks, woven, and cotton sateens adorn every room. The showpiece of the inn, the richly patterned Bridal Suite, displays Chinese silk drapes rescued from El Morocco, the New York nightspot that Angelo Zuccotti once managed.

The house seduces its guests. A long tin bathtub invites visitors to take a luxurious break—bath powder already provided. Seasonal fruit baskets or homemade sweets adorn the rooms as appropriately as the objets d'art and potpourri scents the air.

Innkeepers Angelo and British bred Laura Zuccotti, who was trained at the Cordon Bleu, prepare gourmet fare and present it on elegant china table settings. Snowy white napkins and silver service complete the unabashed indulgence in this Cooperstown showplace.

THE J. P. SILL HOUSE. 63 Chestnut St., Cooperstown, NY 13326; (607) 547-2633; Angelo and Laura Zuccotti, innkeepers. Open all year. 1894 Italiante Victorian with five guest rooms sharing 3½ baths; 1 bridal suite in house and 2-bedroom suite in carriage house (allowing children). Rates: $85 to $225. Two-night minimum for summer weekends June 1 to Oct. 1; 3-night minimum for holiday weekends. Full, elegant breakfast. No pets, kennel nearby; no children under 13; no smoking. Year-round sports activities: Lake Otsego; Baseball Hall of Fame; Farmer's Museum; Fenimore House; antiquing, auctions, summer theatre, and opera.

DIRECTIONS: once in Cooperstown, ask inn for location of the house.

The Garden Room.

ALEXANDER HAMILTON HOUSE

Just 50 minutes from Grand Central

A view, a pool, spacious rooms, and a formal dining room—these were Barbara Notarius's indispensables when searching for the inn of her dreams. The Alexander Hamilton House has them all. Perched on a crest overlooking the Hudson River, the 1889 Victorian crystalized her fantasy.

Stately yet romantic, the five excellent accommodations sport chintz and Laura Ashley, marble-topped chests, hand-carved moldings, and rescued-from-estates antiques. Coupled with the Victoriana are the creature comforts that add to the romance: fireplaces, whirlpool tubs, remote-control television, stereo sound, and an outdoor heated pool.

The Garden Room overlooks the lush gardens in front of the house; the Turret Room boasts five windows in its turret and a winter view of the Hudson; and the Bridal Chamber has five skylights.

A full breakfast is served on the sun-filled porch and delectable hot entrées like blueberry blintzes baked in sour cream sauce, or French toast stuffed with bananas, blueberries, walnuts, or cream cheese are everyone's favorites.

Imagine all this, you city slickers, a mere fifty minutes from Grand Central Station.

ALEXANDER HAMILTON HOUSE, 49 Van Wyck Street, Croton-on-Hudson, NY 10520; (914) 271-6737, Fax (914) 271-3927; Barbara Notarius, owner. Open all year. Four guest rooms and 3 suites, 5 with woodburning fireplaces, all with private baths, cable TV, telephones, air conditioning, ceiling fans. Rates: $75 to $100 single, $95 to $130 double; suites $200 to $250; including full breakfast in sun room or on poolside patio. Well-behaved children welcome ($10 extra in room); no pets; smoking outdoors; Visa/MasterCard/American Express/Discover.

DIRECTIONS: in downtown Croton—call for details. Call ahead for pickup at train.

The 1889 Victorian overlooks the Hudson River.

MOUNTAIN MEADOWS B&B

Just like family

The garden is the center of much activity.

When guests drive through the gates of the Mountain Meadows Bed and Breakfast, all the sights and sounds whet their appetites for the great outdoors. The contemporary home is surrounded by a volley ball net, croquet court, hot tub, swimming pool, gardens, and swings—all within sight of the Shawangunk Mountains (or simply the "Gunks" as known to climbers who come from all over the world to scale these peaks).

Hosts Corinne D'Andrea and Arthur Rifenbary treat arriving guests like family. After showing them to one of the three guest rooms on the first level (all with private baths and king or queen-size beds), travelers can relax by shooting pool in the large recreation room with mountain views. Soon the guests are planning their day, chatting with Corinne and Arthur about mountain climbing, the seventeenth-century stone houses built by the Huguenots in neighboring New Paltz, the excellent restaurants in the area, or about the hiking and cross-country ski trails, golf, and area craft shows. Not to mention that whole yardful of sports and games.

In warm weather Corrine serves breakfast by the pool—egg specialties, waffles, pancakes, fruit, juices, and just-baked muffins.

"We seem to make friends easily with our guests," said Corinne. "Many of them give us hugs when they leave." Just like family.

A guest room.

MOUNTAIN MEADOWS BED & BREAKFAST. 542 Albany Post Road, New Paltz, NY 12561; (914) 255-6144; Corinne D'Andrea and Arthur Rifenbary, hosts. Open all year. Three large guest rooms with queen or king beds. Rates: $85 to $95 single, $95 to $105 double, including big country breakfast. Accepts children and pets "sometimes" (host prefers to discuss this individually with guests at the time of reservation); smoking outdoors only; no credit cards.

DIRECTIONS: exit 18 off NY State Thruway (I-87). Take Rte. 299 west for 4 miles and turn left on Albany Post Road to B&B.

Breakfast treats.

The Spa Suite spa.

INN NEW YORK CITY

Inn-credible

When German *Vogue* touted New York City accommodations in their April, 1993 issue, they mentioned only two: The Ritz Carlton and Inn New York City.

Located on the upper West side, the Inn New York City is a beautifully-pampered brownstone that has been transformed into an artwork by a mother and her daughter. Ruth Mensch, an interior decorator and her daughter, Elyn, a fabric designer, have combined their formidable talents to create a fantasy Victorian world with interiors that are both romantic and dramatic.

The result is four incredible suites. The first floor Parlor Suite, over fifty feet in length, has its own terrace. A king-sized bed with stained-glass headboard and an antique quilt faces a woodburning fireplace. In the center of the room, a Baldwin spinet piano leads to a couch, side chairs, and raised platform for dining. The entire space is abloom with rose-adorned fabrics and carpeting.

The second floor Spa Suite is covered in blues, soft and romantic. A built-in king-sized bed sits on a stepped oak platform. Built-in armoires, a lady's desk, a soft easy chair, and fireplace are just the beginning. In another room, an oversized uniquely decorated spa overwhelms: a generous double Jacuzzi, a sauna, bidet, genuine old barberchair, and a wall cabinet artfully filled with Victorian dolls and bric-a-brac complete the scene.

Two suites, The Vermont, on the ground floor, with a country house feeling and a private entrance, and The Loft Suite, on the third floor, with a fourteen-foot beamed ceiling and sponge-painted guestroom with leaded stained-glass skylight, are captivating.

All of the suites have refrigerators stocked with delicacies from Zabar's and other legendary food palaces. Individual needs are catered to and guests feel like royalty.

INN NEW YORK CITY, (212) 580-1900, Fax (212) 580-4437; Elyn and Ruth Mensch, owners. Open all year. Four suites with private baths, 2 with Jacuzzis. Rates: $195 to $295 per suite, including breakfast. Not suitable for children; no pets; no smoking; Visa/MasterCard/American Express. Near Lincoln Center and Sunday flea market, and limitless choice of restaurants.

DIRECTIONS: off Broadway on Upper West Side. Address provided when making reservations.

Plush and lush.

NYC—SUTTON PLACE

Gilt and elegance

This spacious Sutton Place apartment is furnished as one might expect—*luxuriously*.

Beginning with the marble-floored reception area, the rooms unfold to reveal an elegant décor. A well-polished grand piano, a Scalamandré silk setee, coral-velvet side chairs, a Chinese art deco rug, Louis XVI armchairs, pastoral and floral nineteenth-century oil paintings, and a rosewood game table all command attention. Gilt and elegance are standard fare, and a collection of all-white porcelain china, including Limoges and Wedgewood, is displayed on a coral background.

Two guest rooms, one quite formal and the other furnished in the manner of a den, have private baths appointed with black porcelain and marble fixtures.

A continental breakfast is served each morning by the housekeeper, who will prepare a full breakfast or do your laundry for a small additional fee. All this, plus easy access by taxi to Bloomingdale's, the United Nations, and the Russian Tea Room, makes this location both chic and desirable.

SUTTON PLACE. A luxurious apartment with 2 guest rooms with private baths. Open all year: Rates: $95 for the one guest room, $80 for the other, or $150 for both, including continental breakfast. Children welcome; no pets; smoking allowed; some French spoken; agency accepts Visa/MasterCard/American Express. Directions given upon reservation. Many fine restaurants on nearby 2nd Avenue. *Represented by City Lights Bed & Breakfast Ltd., New York City, (212) 737-7049. Fax (212) 535-2755.*

A richly decorative setting for breakfast.

NYC—GRACIE MANSION AREA

Hob nob with the Mayor

Under the stewardship of a British executive and his charming family, this eclectically-furnished townhouse is just blocks from Gracie Mansion, the home of New York's mayor. It is convenient to the Guggenheim and Metropolitan Museums of Art, and to summer evening concerts overlooking the East River.

A large fireplace dominates the living room and the space resounds with the ambience of a hunting lodge. Add to that a solarium and a rotunda-like dining area with a hanging two-story chandelier, and the effect is completely elegant. English antiques are sprinkled throughout.

The guest rooms are decorated in sensitively coordinated Liberty of London fabrics and wall coverings. Adjoining the rooms is an unusual balcony/library with floor-to-ceiling bookcases and a sumptuous soft leather couch overlooking the rotunda, where breakfast is served.

This upper east side townhouse abounds with good taste.

GRACIE MANSION AREA. A townhouse with 1 guest room and a garden apartment plus another luxurious guest room available occasionally with complimentary French Champagne. Open all year. Rates: $80 guest room, $125 garden apt., $100 special guest room; all include breakfast. Children welcome; no pets; discreet smoking allowed; Spanish, French, some Italian spoken; agency accepts Visa/MasterCard/American Express. Excellent dining in area. *Represented by City Lights Bed & Breakfast Ltd., New York City, (212) 737-7049. Fax (212) 535-2755.*

The Garden Suite.

BEN ASEN

UPPER EAST SIDE

Palatial

Formerly the New Zealand Consulate, this five-story east side townhouse is truly palatial. Complete with a magnificent, imposing staircase and towering crystal chandelier, the formal parlor and dining room are truly grand. The elegant suite on the ground floor is furnished with fine antiques and decorated with choice collectibles. It has access to a lovely garden.

An elevator gently lifts to two elaborately decorated guest rooms on the fifth floor, one with its own terrace overlooking the garden. Purchased in London, wallpapers and fabrics are imaginatively blended. The guest room facing the front of the house has fabric-covered walls and a canopied bed. Every amenity and comfort is provided for.

Breakfast is brought to the room by a housekeeper or may be taken with other guests in a large breakfast room at a round glass table. As one would expect, everything is presented on fine china, set with crystal and silver.

Private dinner parties may be arranged for and there is a special holiday package that includes champagne and holiday gifts.

Bloomingdale's, Tiffany's, Henri Bendel, and Trump Tower are all within blocks.

UPPER EAST SIDE. Two guest rooms with baths and a palatial 1-bedroom suite with bath and kitchen on the garden floor; continental breakfast included, as well as secretarial services and a fax machine. Rates: $170 to $175 per room, $250 suite. Open all year. Inquire about children; no pets; no smoking. Many fine restaurants in immediate area. *Represented by City Lights Bed & Breakfast Ltd.*, P.O. Box 20355 Cherokee Station, New York, NY 10028; (212) 737-7049, FAX (212) 535-2755; Visa/MasterCard/American Express/Diners/Carte Blanche.

DIRECTIONS: given on reservation.

BEN ASEN

A Greek Revival interior with intricate Corinthian columns.

THE BARTLETT HOUSE INN

Beachside Victoriana

If you have ever wished you had an old family country house by the sea, then this inn will suit your reveries. The Bartlett House is a spacious late-Victorian with the casual style of a beach home, the kind of place where antiques and sea breezes live in harmony. An extra-wide front porch greets visitors to the bed and breakfast, and the roomy dimensions are carried on inside. The front parlor sports Corinthian columns by its doorways and an ornately carved fireplace. A grand staircase leads to the two floors above, with light streaming in through leaded-glass windows.

Guest rooms are welcoming, with brass beds and white chenille bedspreads. Rocking chairs, patchwork quilts and patterned rugs lend a cozy feel to each room. Innkeeper Linda Sabatino has a great eye for small collectibles, and you'll see the evidence in the many small lamps, tables, and curios that give the rooms their character. And everywhere in the house, from the dining room on up to the nooks and crannies of the third floor rooms, you'll find seashells arranged on ledges or tabletops.

The Bartlett House is in the center of Greenport, a former whaling town on the quiet North Fork of Eastern Long Island. A beach is located at the end of the street, and sailing, fishing, and canoeing are all available. The village is perfect for strolling or bicycling. Daytrips to Shelter Island, via the ferry in town, are a popular activity, where a nature preserve offers hiking trails. Antiquing, tennis, and golf are also nearby. Innkeeper John Sabatino recommends a visit to some of the acclaimed vineyards in the area for tours and tastings. "But," adds your host, "the most popular activity out here is just relaxing."

THE BARTLETT HOUSE INN, 503 Front Street, Greenport, Long Island, NY 11944; (516) 477-0371; John and Linda Sabatino, owners. Open all year. Nine guest rooms, including 1 suite, all with private baths and air conditioning. Rates: $79 to $100 in season, $67 to $86 off season, per room. Single is $5 less. Includes full breakfast, buffet style. Children over 12 welcome; no pets; smoking limited; all credit cards. Variety of casual to formal dining nearby.

DIRECTIONS: Long Island Railroad and buses to town depot. Arrangements to meet ferry from Connecticut at Orient Point. Ask for car directions.

Owner Elsie Collins.

The 100-year-old converted red barn.

1880 HOUSE B&B

A Hampton treasure

Ideally situated on Westhampton Beach's exclusive Seafield Lane, Elsie Collins' 1880 House is a local treasure. Crammed with antiquities and the family mementos of past generations, it harkens back to the bygone days of a "visit to grandmother."

Lovingly preserved are Victorian lounges, an apothecary chest, a pot belly stove, needlework, Shaker benches, hurricane lamps, and Chinese and English porcelain.

Two suites are available in the main house: the Victorian Blue Suite with delicate floral wallpaper and raised brass bed, or the more rustic paneled Yellow Suite with a love seat, antique oak desk, and floral-painted claw-foot tub. Both suites have their own sitting rooms and baths, antique coverlets, and delicately embroidered pillow cases. Another country suite is located in the hundred-year-old restored barn and has its own kitchen for "playing house" as well as a sunken tub.

There is a pool on the premises for a late-night dip, and the beach is just six blocks away. The center

Left above, the parlor, with a 19th-century apothecary chest. Below, Kim's Suite.

of town, just two blocks away, has a good selection of restaurants. Elsie Collins' 1880 House is a place to unwind from the workaday world and to find restoration.

1880 HOUSE BED & BREAKFAST. 2 Seafield Lane, P.O. Box 648, Westhampton Beach, NY 11978; (800) 346-3290, (516) 288-1559, Fax (516) 288-0721; Elsie Collins, owner. Open all year. Three suites, 2 in main house, one in converted barn, all with private baths, air conditioning, and TVs. Rates: $150 to $200; $100 from Labor Day to Memorial Day. Includes full breakfast. Inquire about children and pets; no smoking; Visa/MasterCard/American Express. Tennis court and swimming pool on premises. Five blocks from beach, 2 blocks from town center and restaurants.

DIRECTIONS: take Long Island Expressway exit 70 south to Rte. 27 east to Westhampton. Call inn for directions from there.

The original farmhouse, built in 1880.

NEW JERSEY

BARNARD-GOOD HOUSE

They wrote the book on breakfast

Early morning always finds Nan Hawkins bustling about her roomy kitchen, preparing a tableful of delicious surprises for her guests. Nan's reputation as a cook has spread to national magazines and major newspapers that have featured her morning treats. She has even written her own cookbook, *Why Not For Breakfast?* with dozens of her recipes.

While there may be larger and more elaborate Victorian bed and breakfasts in Cape May (a National Historic Landmark city with over 600 Victorian houses), Nan's breakfasts are notable attractions. When guests arrive in the afternoon, they are greeted with hot or iced tea and cookies before beginning their exploration of the house. The living room is filled with Victorian antiques and surprises, from a boat on the mantel, made by Nan's father, to an early oil painting of the house before the Hawkinses restored it, to an ancient mahogany piano. Look again at that old sheet music ready to be played: "On the Way to Cape May."

Each of the guest rooms has its own sense of fun and history. In one bathroom is a copper tub for ablutions from bygone days; in another room, a dressing table and mirror framed by a fluffy lace hood and skirt.

Some guests enjoy sitting in the wicker chairs on the wide front porch with a row of American flags flapping in the sea breeze. The Atlantic ocean and a swimming beach are just two blocks away.

Left above, one of Cape May's painted ladies. Below, the parlor has a turn-of-the-century look.

Tom and Nan Hawkins, owners, with their cookbook.

BARNARD-GOOD HOUSE. 238 Perry St., Cape May, NJ 08204; (609) 884-5381; Tom and Nan Hawkins, owners. Open April 1 to November 1. Two suites (sitting room, bedroom, and bath) and three guest rooms, all with private baths. Rates $90 to $130 double, 10% discount for singles. Includes four-course breakfast, a "hallmark of the house." Children over 14 welcome; no pets; smoking on veranda only; Visa/MasterCard. Hosts supply beach tags, beach chairs, and towels.

DIRECTIONS: go to mile marker "0" at the end of Garden State Parkway, then over Canal Bridge to Lafayette Street. Turn right at end of this street and go to the next traffic light. Drive through the open gate and park on the property.

An inviting sitting area.

One of the colorful guest rooms.

Left, fun and games, Victorian style.

THE ABBEY

Casual elegance

One of the more elaborate carpenter gothic houses in Cape May is a seaside villa built in 1869 by a wealthy coal baron who spared no expense in creating an architectural masterpiece for entertaining summer guests at the sea shore. Now transformed into a bed and breakfast of expansive proportions by Jay and Marianne Schatz, the building has been delightfully restored. The interior contains a variety of decorative Victorian wallpaper reproductions as a setting for a collection of nineteenth-century furniture and bric-a-brac that brings the period back to life in a charming way.

An adjacent building, The Cottage, was recently added to the inn. Built in 1873 for the coal baron's son, it is a delightful empire style home with bright airy rooms furnished with choice antiques.

Croquet on the lawn, with the men wearing straw boaters; afternoon tea on the porch, including the hosts leading stimulating conversation with the guests; music played on an antique harp or an 1850 square grand piano in the parlor, which functions essentially as a music room; all these add to the atmosphere of life in another time—less hurried, less hectic, less harrowing.

Cape May is the nation's oldest seaside resort, and a stroll along its tree-lined, gaslit streets at dusk on a summer's evening recreates the heyday of the nineteenth century: ice cream parlors, Sousa brass bands, bicycles, carriages, knickered boys, hoops, and the backdrop to it all, the incredible collection of hundreds of extravagantly ornamented Victorian houses built in Italianate and Gothic Revival styles, among which The Abbey stands out.

THE ABBEY, Columbia Avenue and Gurney Street, Cape May, NJ 08204; (609) 884-4506; Jay and Marianne Schatz, Hosts. Open April through November. Fourteen rooms, all with private baths in two adjacent houses (some with air conditioners). Rates: $90 to $175 per couple; includes full breakfast in spring and fall, lighter buffet in summer, and afternoon refreshments through the year, and onsite parking for main house. No liquor served; guests may bring their own. Well-behaved children over 12 welcome; no pets; all smoking limited to the veranda; Visa/MasterCard/Discover. Croquet at the inn, seashore swimming one block away, and many other activities.

DIRECTIONS: in Cape May, turn left on Ocean street, drive 3 blocks and turn left on Columbia Avenue. The inn is one block down.

MANOR HOUSE INN

Engaging innkeepers in Cape May

Cape May's Hughes Street is lined with gracious homes and lush shade trees, and it is one of the choicest addresses in the village. To make matters complete, the street is centrally located between the shops and restaurants of the pedestrian mall and the ocean beach.

One of the most relaxed and engaging places to stay along this tranquil byway is the Manor House, ably operated by Tom and Nancy McDonald. Juxtaposed with the gingerbread opulence of many nearby inns, the Manor House is comparatively modest and unassuming. This inn is a spacious, three-story Colonial Revival home, iced with weathered shingles, capped with a gambrel roof, and girded in front by an old-fashioned "sitting" porch—a favorite hang-out during the balmy days of summer. Inside, everything is spit-and-polish perfection.

MANOR HOUSE INN, 612 Hughes Street, Cape May. NJ 08204; (609) 884-4710; Tom and Nancy McDonald, owners. Open Feb. 1 to Dec. 31. Nine rooms, 7 with private baths and 2 sharing 1 bath. Rates: $79 to $166. Children over 12 welcome; no pets; major credit cards accepted. Traditional seafood and "creative cuisine" restaurants in area.

DIRECTIONS: from bridge into Cape May follow Lafayette St. for 8 blocks to Franklin and turn left for 2 blocks to Hughes. Turn right. If street parking is full, pull into driveway next to sign.

The Queen Victoria Room is appropriately regal.

THE QUEEN VICTORIA

Imposing Victorian on Cape May

The Queen Victoria ranks among the best of Cape May's many distinctive bed and breakfast inns. It towers on the corner of Ocean Street and Columbia Avenue, a dramatic green and maroon gingerbread cottage. Owners Joan and Dane Wells are perfectly suited to the task of pampering this Victorian lady. Before beginning a career as an innkeeper, Joan was curator of the Molly Brown House in Denver as well as the executive director of The Victorian Society. Both positions required a dedication to the preservation of old houses, a labor Joan truly loves. Dane is the perfect counterpart. Though a tinkerer and hardware store aficionado, his professional background in retailing keeps the inn's business side on an even keel.

One of the most attractive and interesting rooms in the entire house is the front parlor, which is filled with the Wellses' Arts and Crafts furniture collection—that wonderfully subdued offspring of the gaudy Victorian age.

Bedrooms come in many shapes and sizes. On the first floor the Queen Victoria room handily houses a massive armoire, tufted couch, king-size bed, and petit point chairs. Several rooms on the second floor and all on the third are diminutive and charming. The Wellses carefully selected wallpapers to suit the spirit of Victoriana, each with jewel-like hues and intricate patterns.

Though Cape May is a wonderful place to visit, no matter the season, the Wellses favorite time of year is Christmas. To make the season more joyous, they organize caroling, fireside readings from Dickens, and workshop sessions devoted to planning the Victorian Christmas dinner and decorating the Victorian home.

THE QUEEN VICTORIA, 102 Ocean St., Cape May, NJ 08204; (609) 884-8702; Dane and Joan Wells, hosts. French and some Spanish spoken. Open all year, minimum stays vary seasonally. Seventeen guest rooms and 7 suites, all with private baths. Rates: $80 to $200 per room, $160 to $250 per suite according to size and amenities (rates lower off season), including full breakfast served buffet style. Afternoon tea. Excellent dining nearby. Children in suites only; no pets; no smoking; Visa/MasterCard.

DIRECTIONS: take Garden State Pkwy. to Cape May, where it becomes Lafayette St. Turn left at second stoplight (Ocean St.) and proceed three blocks to inn, on right.

The first and most honored bed and breakfast in Cape May.

THE MAINSTAY INN

Bed and breakfast at its best

The heyday of Cape May as one of the premier resort towns on the East Coast coincided with the height of Victorian carpenter craftsmanship in the latter part of the nineteenth century, and Cape May has hundreds of finely crafted, exquisitely detailed gingerbread houses to prove it.

One of these, an Italianate former gaming house built in 1872, was restored to its former glory by Tom and Sue Carroll, who have made the Mainstay into the best known bed and breakfast in the East. Because of their painstaking search for authenticity in the recreation of Victorian interiors, their inn has become a highly respected and much-loved model for other innkeepers aspiring to recreate the same sort of ambiance.

The interior of the inn is a unique combination of lush, Persian and Oriental rugs, wonderfully decorative Bradbury and Bradbury period wallpapers and mouldings, elaborate details in the form of paintings, china, drapes, lamps, quilts, chandeliers, clocks, vases, and, finally, an overwhelming collection of Victorian antique furniture. Guest rooms contain giant beds with decorative foot and head boards, intricately carved wardrobes, dressers, and washstands with marble tops, and velvet upholstered chairs and settees. The public rooms contain more: giant pier mirrors, elaborately upholstered walnut and mahogany chairs and settees, and exotic divans.

Amidst this Victorian flamboyance, the perfectly modern young innkeepers maintain an air of calm and serenity throughout the two guest houses. Guests meet each other over the delicious full breakfasts and during afternoon tea, oftentimes served on the Mainstay's ample porch.

THE MAINSTAY INN, 635 Columbia Avenue, Cape May, NJ 08204; (609) 884-8690; Tom and Sue Carroll, hosts. Open all year in one building; in others mid-March through mid-December. Sixteen rooms in 3 buildings, all with private baths. Rates: $135 to $250 in season; includes full breakfast in spring and fall, Continental in summer on veranda; afternoon tea. No liquor served; guests may bring their own. Children over 6 in one building; in others over 12 welcome; no pets; smoking on veranda only; no credit cards. Croquet and swimming at the seashore.

DIRECTIONS: 2 blocks from Convention Hall in the center of town.

MARLA C. BERGER PHOTOGRAPHS

An extravagantly wallpapered Victorian guest room.

HUMPHREY HUGHES HOUSE

A doctor's home

Open year-round and presided over by charming hosts Lorraine and Terry Schmidt, The Humphrey Hughes House provides gracious accommodations. Bedecked in Victorian finery, the grand house is stuffed with treasures that belonged to the Hughes family, whose place in Cape May history was secured in 1692, when Captain Humphrey Hughes arrived

The richly paneled entrance hall.

to become one of its original landowners. This house, erected in 1903, and home to Dr. Franklin Hughes, remained in the family's hands until his son, Dr. Harold Hughes, died in 1980.

The Velvet Room, a guest room which was formerly the medical library, still houses medical books and medical instruments in elegant surroundings of carved oak and ruby-red glass. Another of the ten guest rooms, The Rose Room, has rose-silk walls, a damask fainting couch, and original gas fixtures.

Velvet and brocade-covered furniture, Victorian sculpted figures, lace-covered swags, and a mahogany square baby grand, all fan the senses. Add to that the wonderful ocean views, an elegant breakfast, two crackling fireplaces, and a glassed-in sun porch.

THE HUMPHREY HUGHES HOUSE, 29 Ocean Street, Cape May, NJ 08204; (800) 582-3634, (609) 884-4428; Lorraine and Terry Schmidt, owners. Open all year. Seven guest rooms and 4 suites, with private baths, cable TV in suites, air conditioning in all rooms. Rates: $118 to $155 double, $150 to $215 for suites. Includes full sit-down breakfast and afternoon tea with goodies. No children; no pets; smoking on porches only; Visa/MasterCard. In heart of Cape May.

DIRECTIONS: follow Lafayette Street right downtown to Ocean St. and turn left to inn several blocks down on left.

Some of John Peto's paintings, including a self-portrait on the easel.

THE STUDIO OF JOHN F. PETO

A secluded artist's studio

Gifted in the art of still life, John F. Peto, who lived during the latter half of the nineteenth century, was an artist whose talent was to go unrecognized in his lifetime. Throughout his career, he was unfavorably compared to friend and fellow painter William Michael Harnett. In 1950 the tide began to turn when the Brooklyn Museum mounted Peto's first major exhibition. Thirty-three years later when the National Gallery of Art organized a retrospective that traveled from Washington, D.C. to the Amon Carter Museum in Fort Worth, Texas, Peto finally emerged as a major American painter, now considered by many to be a far greater talent than Harnett.

Peto lived his life in virtual seclusion in Island Heights, a quiet village along the New Jersey shore, in a house he built overlooking the Tom's River. He first designed a studio for himself, a spacious and high-ceilinged room with white stuccoed fireplace, white walls, and "Peto red" wainscoting. He then built his home, including seven bedrooms, around the studio.

Granddaughter Joy Peto Smiley, as ebullient as her forebears were reclusive, has opened her grandfather's home and studio to overnight guests. Rooms are furnished much as they always have been, unpretentious with an eclectic mix of beds, chest, and chairs. In the common rooms hang reproductions of Peto's most famous paintings, and the studio holds a small selection of his original works.

Whether dining on Joy's "ethereal eggs," fresh fruit, and hot popovers, or walking through historic Island Heights, the studio, filled with the strong and quiet presence of John Peto, is the most memorable part of a stay.

THE STUDIO OF JOHN F. PETO, 102 Cedar Ave., Island Heights, NJ 08732; (908) 270-6058; Joy Peto Smiley, hostess. Open year-round. Four air conditioned guest rooms with shared baths. Rates: $55 to $100, including hearty breakfast. Variety of restaurants, including many wonderful seafood eateries in the area. Children twelve and over; no pets; American Express, personal checks.

DIRECTIONS: take Garden State Pkwy. to exit 82 east. Pass through six stoplights. Two blocks further, turn right onto Central Ave. and drive ¼ mile; halfway up the first hill, turn left onto Summit. Drive 4 blocks and turn right onto Cedar. Inn is 2 blocks on left (look for sign "The Studio").

The billiard room.

A decorative guest room.

NORTHWOOD INN

Shipshape accommodations

When this Queen Anne-style Victorian was built in Ocean City in 1894, it was the northernmost structure on the island. Flanked by woods to the north and sand dunes in its backyard stretching east to the Atlantic Ocean, today the woods and dunes have been transformed into houses and resorts, but the ocean is still only three short blocks away.

John Loeper and his wife Marj fell in love with the Ocean City island and with the house. They saw many possibilities in the gracious old Victorian and began a complete restoration, officially opening the house as the Northwood Inn in 1990. John had owned a shipyard in Connecticut, and his avocation had long been model boat building. He used all these skills in crafting a unique English telephone booth for guests in the foyer, creating models of boats for the library and living room, and adding such guest-pleasing touches as a pool table. Marj's presence can be seen in flower signs on all the guest room doors (each named for a different flower). The Lotus Blossom Suite offers a queen-size bed and a separate sitting room with full pull-out sofa. The Tulip Room has a queen-size bed and a private full bath.

Marj and John serve a continental breakfast on weekdays (with muffins, fruit, juices, coffee, tea) and a full breakfast on weekends. "I take some pride in selecting and serving some of the freshest melons and other fruit," said John.

Left, your host, John Loeper.

Guests can enjoy all the pleasures of two miles of boardwalk and eight miles of beaches (free beach tags are supplied by your hosts). Many guests also visit Atlantic City, about a fifteen-minute drive from the inn.

NORTHWOOD INN. 401 Wesley Ave., Ocean City, NJ 08226; (609) 399-6071; John and Marj Loeper, owners. Open all year. Seven guest rooms and one suite, all with private baths. Rates: $90 to $150 per room, include a continental breakfast on weekdays, full breakfast on weekends. No children under 10, no pets; smoking on exterior porches only; Visa/MasterCard/American Express.

DIRECTIONS: take exit 30 off Garden State Parkway and follow Ocean City signs. In Ocean City take a left onto Wesley.

The Queen Anne style inn.

The library.

SEA CREST BY THE SEA

Play it again, Sam

"A lovingly restored 1885 Queen Anne Victorian for ladies and gentlemen on seaside holiday." Those words could have been written late in the nineteenth Century, shortly after Spring Lake, New Jersey was "discovered" by wealthy families from Philadelphia and New York. But they appear today on the business cards of John and Carol Kirby, innkeepers of Sea Crest by the Sea.

When John retired as world-traveling president of a bio-medical firm, he wanted a real change of pace in his life. He and Carol decided to create a quiet, Victorian escape for couples in incredibly luxurious surroundings, in a bed and breakfast with eleven antique-laden guest rooms and one suite. Each of the rooms spins its own idyllic fantasy.

If you want to reminisce about one of the most romantic movies of all time, slide the beaded curtains aside and enter the 1940's Casablanca room, decorated with memorabilia of the famous Ingrid Bergman-Humphrey Bogart classic film. There's even a copy of the original script and a Bogart-style raincoat draped over a trunk that must be filled with intrigue.

Left above, the imposing building in all its splendor. Below, the ornate dining room.

SEA CREST BY THE SEA, 19 Tuttle Ave., Spring Lake, NJ 07762; (800) 803-9031 or (908) 449-4031; John and Carol Kirby, hosts. Eleven rooms, one suite, all with queen beds, private baths, phones, TV/VCR. Some have working gas fireplaces and ocean views. Rates: $115 to $189 (rooms); $195 to $249 (suite). Gourmet breakfast and high tea included. No children; no pets; smoking confined to outside porch; Visa/MasterCard/American Express. Collection of menus from many excellent area restaurants in the library. Nearby activities include swimming, birding, biking, antiquing, golf, and tennis.

DIRECTIONS: from New York and north, take Garden State Parkway to exit 98 to Rte. 34 south to the first traffic circle and east on to Rte. 524 east. Turn right on Ocean Avenue to Tuttle. From Philadelphia and south, take I-195 east and exit to Rte. 34 south. Follow above directions.

The Casablanca Room has a trunk covered with memorabilia.

Or soak in a huge tub in the Teddy Roosevelt Suite, watching movies on TV.

Breakfast is served at the "civilized" hour of 9 A.M. in a magnificent dining room suitable for visiting Rockefellers and Vanderbilts. The gourmet repast always includes the hostess's famous buttermilk scones, several warm dishes, and a coffee blended specially for Sea Crest.

Afterwards, guests can play croquet on a wide lawn, or borrow a bike from a nearby rack and take a ride along a beautiful two-mile beach from miraculously free of such modern-day detritus as fast food restaurants and T-shirt shops.

The Teddy Roosevelt Suite is filled with teddy bears.

The largest, most imposing guest room.

THE NORMANDY INN

Gracious privacy a block from the beach

Of all the seaside villages that attract vacationers to the New Jersey shore, none is more gracious than Spring Lake. Bypassed by the teeming hordes who populate streets, casinos, and beaches of larger resorts, Spring Lake emanates a special grace particular to communities made up of broad avenues lined with grand, tree-shaded "cottages."

Built in 1888 as a private residence and expanded in 1909, The Normandy Inn, which comprises eighteen bedrooms, sits one block from the beach. Size alone makes the Normandy feel like a small resort hotel, though innkeepers Susan and Michael Ingino, who live in the house year-round with daughter Beth, maintain a warm and homey atmosphere.

Breakfast at this inn is especially generous and delicious. Each morning guests seat themselves in the large dining room—a room of such scale that young Beth dreams of converting it into her own private skating rink. The written menu offers many choices. Besides the requisite juices, hot beverages, and cold cereals, the Inginos serve real Irish porridge, four types of pancakes, two sorts of French toast, six varieties of eggs, four breakfast meats, and Michael's fresh-baked muffins or soda bread. Breakfast is Michael's favorite meal, and as a chef, he sees to it that guests need eat but a sparing lunch.

The Inginos are avid collectors of Victoriana and have furnished each room with antiques and details from the period. Rooms vary in size, but each is clean and very comfortable.

THE NORMANDY INN, 21 Tuttle Ave., Spring Lake, NJ 07762; (908) 449-7172, Fax (908) 449-1070; Michael and Susan Ingino, hosts. Italianate Victorian home near beach offers casual comfort and thoughtful amenities. Open all year. 18 guest rooms in main house, including one suite, 1 suite in Carriage House; all with private baths. Rates $108 to $161 in season, $86 to $129 off season, double occupancy. Includes full breakfast. Good dining throughout area. Children who enjoy quietude welcome; no pets; smoking discouraged; all major credit cards.

DIRECTIONS: from north, take Garden State Pkwy. to exit 98 (Rte. 34). Proceed south on 34 to traffic circle. Drive ¾ way around and turn right on Rte. 524 east. Cross Rtes. 35 and 71. Rte. 524 then becomes Ludlow Ave. Proceed to end of Ludlow and turn right onto Ocean Ave., then first right onto Tuttle. From south, take Garden State Pkwy. to exit 98 (Rte. 38 E). Cross Rte. 18 and turn right at next traffic light onto New Bedford Rd. Take sharp left at second stop sign (Rte. 524) and proceed as above.

CONOVER'S BAY HEAD INN

The pearl of seaside inns

Beverly Conover's light touch and delicate sense of color reveal an exquisite aesthetic sensitivity that defines the inn—from the embracing warm tones of lavender and mauve on the first floor to the family photographs she has framed and placed in each room.

Every one of the twelve dignified bedrooms has a distinct personality. The brightest room is also the most dramatic. Splashes of red and green in the geranium wallpaper match the brilliant red of the table skirt and ruffled cushion on the white wicker settee. In another room, a smoke-blue and white Laura Ashley print on the wall is reversed on the chair upholstery. In yet another, a spool bed and curly maple dresser are paired with pink and lime linens, a green stenciled border, and a row of small porcelain ducks that nest on top of the window sill.

The views are equally impressive. The sinuously curved maple bed in one third-floor room is placed so that reclining guests can see the bay, marina, and yacht club. Reflections of the ocean gleam in other rooms. Shapely old-style shingle houses comprise the rest of the scenic landscape.

Bay Head captures the feel of a late nineteenth-century residential summer village. The few, quaint shops sell antiques, art wear, prints, books, gifts, and clothing. Very little tells of life's more pressing necessities. "Which is as it should be," notes Beverly.

"I like to fuss. I always fuss over breakfast," Beverly adds. Inspired baked goods grace the table as beautifully as the place settings. Fresh-squeezed orange juice and cut fruit are part of the full breakfast served every day. Guests can dine in the sunny breakfast room, on the manicured lawn, or on the front porch.

Conover's is a classic among bed and breakfasts, the pearl of seaside inns.

CONOVER'S BAY HEAD INN, 646 Main Ave., Bay Head, NJ 08742; (908) 892-4664; Carl and Beverly Conover, hosts. Open all year. Summer cottage built in 1905 and located one block from the beach. Twelve guest rooms, all with private baths. Rates: $110 to $210 weekends (weekdays less) in season; off-season discounts; singles $10 less double rate. Full breakfast included. Tea served in the afternoons until May 1. Children aged 13 and up are welcome in July and August only; no pets; outdoor smoking; American Express/MasterCard/Visa. Lawn games; golf; tennis; winter sports on Twilight Lake; beach; windsurfing.

DIRECTIONS: from the Garden State Parkway, take Rte. 34 (exit 98) and follow signs for Rte. 35. Continue on Rte. 35 south into Bay Head. The inn is on the right.

A farmhouse guest room with a wood fireplace.

RED MAPLE FARM

The bed and breakfast that went to Princeton

Roberta Churchill was the chef and owner of a Princeton restaurant rated one of the five best in New Jersey by no less an authority than *The New York Times.* Her husband Lindsey was a Fulbright Scholar who studied in Finland and now is a sociology professor at a New York City college.

What better backgrounds could a couple have for running a bed and breakfast that is also a two-and-a-half acre mini-farm with historic buildings dating back to 1740! They own and manage the Red Maple Farm, just four miles from the main gate of Princeton University. Roberta also has a passion for folk art that bedecks walls and tables throughout the house— Navaho, Finnish, and Peruvian wall hangings, Tibetan petit-point, rugs from Georgia in the former Soviet Union, and bird carvings from the Caribbean and France.

Staying at the Red Maple Farm is an unending

Left above, the farmhouse built in 1740. Below, owner Lindsey Churchill relaxing in the garden swimming pool.

delight. Roberta serves up her egg frittata, scones, and other home-made specialties using ingredients fresh from her farm garden. She serves this country breakfast in the dining room, with logs burning in the fireplace on winter mornings. She and Lindsey frequently join guests in conversations with topics that can range from travel and art to current world trends. Guests are free to roam the grounds, take a dip in the flower-lined swimming pool a few yards from the house, and enjoy the fine shops and restaurants of Princeton.

The farmhouse, surrounded by oak, poplar, and of course, red maples, is on the National Historic Register and contains many surprises. A tunnel was uncovered several years ago that led from the house to the barn, suggesting that the house could have been a station on the Underground Railway that helped protect runaway slaves. A "secret room" discovered in the farmhouse with yellowing Civil War era newspapers supports this theory.

RED MAPLE FARM. RD 4 Raymond Road, Princeton, NJ, 08540; (908) 329-3821; Lindsey and Roberta Churchill, owners. Open all year. Three guest rooms with semi-private baths. Rates: $55 to $75 per room with a $10 supplement for one night weekend stays; includes full country breakfast. Children over 6 welcome; no pets; no smoking; Visa/MasterCard/American Express. Cross-country skiing, canoeing, and indoor or outdoor tennis nearby in season.

DIRECTIONS: four miles from Princeton University. Call for specific directions.

THE WHISTLING SWAN INN

Fit for the society pages

In 1905, when the local justice of the peace finished building his gracious Queen Anne Victorian home, he threw a party that was noted in the society pages of the *Stanhope Eagle*. Almost a century later, the splendidly-restored Victorian is The Whistling Swan Inn. Thanks to its owners Paula Williams and Joe Mulay, it is once again fit for the society pages.

The ten-room bed and breakfast is located in the quiet town of Stanhope, less than an hour away from New York City. High-ceilinged rooms and wide hallways create an aura of peacefulness. Especially serene is the third-floor suite. Its bedroom, in the turret of the house, has a cathedral ceiling and a series of etched windows.

The décor is mostly country-Victorian, making use of rich colors and textures. Each guest room has a theme, such as 1920s era, or Oriental Victorian, and much of the furniture came from Paula's family. The ruby-red parlor is welcoming, with its player piano and carafe of sherry.

While each room has a private bath, a unique amenity offered to all guests of The Whistling Swan is *Tubs for Two*—a large sun-dappled bathroom complete with two deep claw-footed tubs, a selection of bubble baths, and an armoire full of fluffy robes.

THE WHISTLING SWAN INN, 110 Main Street, P.O. Box 791, Stanhope, NJ 07874; (201) 347-6369, Fax (201) 347-3391; Paula Williams and Joe Mulay, owners. Open all year. Ten guest rooms with private baths, queen beds, and central air conditioning. Rates: (per room) Nov. through April $75 to $100, May through Oct. $85 to $110, including full breakfast served buffet style. Children 12 and over welcome; no pets; smoking on porch only; all credit cards accepted. All outdoor activities available, plus special events such as jazz and poetry festivals and major musical performances at Waterloo Village 2 miles away; antiquing and winery visits.

DIRECTIONS: from Rte. 80 take exit 27 north onto Rte. 183 for 1 mile to Hoss Building and turn left.

CHESTNUT HILL ON THE DELAWARE

Old-fashioned and very romantic

Visitors to Linda and Rob Castagna's home, Chestnut Hill, are enveloped by the warmth of the atmosphere and the beauty of the setting on the banks of the Delaware.

Bedrooms are old-fashioned and very romantic, thanks to Linda's gift for color and design and her many small touches. On the door of each room hangs a delicate wreath, and inside a handcrafted cloth basket is filled with fresh fruit in season. One room, entitled Peaches and Cream, is an aptly named chamber with soft peach-striped wallpaper, puffy peach comforter draped with a lace coverlet, and an oak chest of drawers and armoire. The Pineapple Room, which was the servants quarters, is roomy and private at the rear of the second floor. Decorated in cream, yellows, and greens, the room offers a bed dressed with a luxurious Welsh duvet and a wall of built-in drawers and cabinets in which hides a television. Bayberry features a bay window fitted with original shutters and is decorated in sprightly primary shades taken from colors in the bed's antique quilt.

Up a steep staircase to the attic suite, the bridal favorite, guests are in a world of their own. One bedroom is named Teddy's Place and contains several furry bears and a Little Golden Book of the *Three Bears* tale. Against a warm and rosy red print wallpaper, white eyelet and ruffled bedclothes look crisp and inviting. The bathroom, which displays beautiful Italian tile work, overlooks the swift-flowing Delaware.

CHESTNUT HILL ON THE DELAWARE, 63 Church St., Milford, NJ 08848; (908) 995-9761; Linda and Rob Castagna, hosts. Victorian house built in 1860, with gallery/gift shop on premises. Open year-round. Five guest rooms, shared and private baths; honeymoon country cottage. Rates: $85 to $140, two night minimum on weekends. Full breakfast served, fixings in cottage. Excellent dining in area. No pets; no smoking; checks accepted.

DIRECTIONS: from Milford, turn right at light and right again on Church St. (1 street before Delaware River bridge). Turn left into dead-end, which is Chestnut Hill's parking area.

CHIMNEY HILL FARM

Countryside tranquility

Chimney Hill Farm was built originally in 1820 as a small, stone farm house, with a sweeping view of the Delaware River Valley and Bucks County, Pennsylvania. Over the years it grew into a country estate and is now a gracious bed and breakfast.

The tone is set upon entering the formal living room with its dark hardwood floors, traditional antique furniture, hunting prints, and collection of cut crystal. Guest rooms are similarly filled with a mixture of antiques and period reproductions. The Hunt Room, named for the lawyer who once owned the place, is cheerily done in traditionally patterned fabrics of red, coral, and green, and features an elegant canopied bed. The Campaign Room makes use of more contemporary fabrics on a gun-metal steel reproduction of the canopied beds officers used to take to war with them. Faux marbling on the walls lends an artful touch to this original room.

A favorite gathering place for guests is a large sun room, with light streaming in, or with the fireplace aglow. Gardens surround the farm house, perfect for a stroll, and families of deer sometimes wander within view of the windows. A full breakfast is served in the dining room at candlelit tables for two, or around a larger table for the more sociable. Delicious raspberry jam, from berries grown on the property, and a morning newspaper always accompany the breakfast.

A feeling of quiet gentility permeates Chimney Hill Farm, complemented by the wide views of the countryside. Popular activities include hot air ballooning and attending the annual Amwell Hunt.

CHIMNEY HILL FARM, RD 3, Box 150, Lambertville, NJ 08530; (609) 397-1516, Fax (609) 397-9353; Terry Ann and Richard Anderson, owners. Open all year. Eight rooms with private baths, including 3 kings, 4 queens. Rates: $110 to $155 per room, including full breakfast; special mid-week rates. No children; no pets; no smoking; Visa/MasterCard/American Express. Antiquing and shopping in New Hope; downhill skiing at Belle Mountain Ski Area day or night; hot air ballooning, kyaking, bicycling, tubing. DIRECTIONS: call.

JERICA HILL

Restored to match childhood memories

When Judith Studer was a child growing up in Flemington, New Jersey, she visited this old Victorian home that belonged to her best friend's grandfather.

It had been built by a local businessman who owned a neighboring lumberyard, and no effort had been spared in fitting the generously proportioned rooms with the finest woods. Five years ago she bought it, by then in a state of total disrepair. Lovingly she has restored it to match her wonderful childhood memories of gleaming hardwood floors and finely polished intricate woodwork. The exterior has been painted to reflect her own vibrant vision of Jerica Hill—a vivid gray with burgundy shutters and soft pearl gray trim.

The guest rooms have been named after Judith's relatives who lived in the area. Period pieces adorn each of the distinctive rooms: wicker and brass, oak, antique pine, and formal mahogony furniture. Antique spreads, coverlets, and country quilts dress up the beds. Lots of family pieces and things gathered up from the area appear throughout. Each guest room is supplied with fresh flowers, fruit, and sparkling water.

Born into the hostelry business, Judith grew up with parents who owned Flemington's historic Union Hotel, across the street from where the Lindbergh trial was held in the 1930's. For more than four generations her family has lived and worked in the area.

If you were born to shop, the town is awash with better than eighty outlets including Flemington Furs, Calvin Klein, Villeroy & Boch, and Waterford crystal. Many are within walking distance. When you are tired of shopping, Judith can arrange for a Champagne hot air balloon flight or picnic tours of the wineries in the beautiful Delaware River Valley.

JERICA HILL, 96 Broad Street, Flemington, NJ 08822; (908) 782-8234; Judith S. Studer, innkeeper. Open all year. Five guest rooms with private baths, telephones, air conditioning. Rates: $80 to $105 double. Includes expanded continental breakfast. Inquire about children; no pets; no smoking; Visa/MasterCard/American Express. Two cats on premises. Hot-air balloon flights and winery tours of Delaware River Valley arranged here. Outlet shopping galore in Flemington's "Liberty Village." Bucks County nearby.

DIRECTIONS: from US-202 traveling north or south proceed to US-202/Rte. 31 traffic circle to Rte. 31 north off circle. At first traffic light turn left onto Church St. and proceed 2 blocks to Broad St. Turn right and continue 2 blocks to 96 Broad St.

Innkeepers Pam Venosa and Al Scott.

THE CABBAGE ROSE INN

As fanciful as a wedding cake

Splendidly asymmetrical, this Queen Anne Victorian presides over Main Street like a fanciful wedding cake. This seems appropriate, as owners Pam Venosa and Al Scott were themselves married here in 1988, the day before they opened the restored mansion as a bed and breakfast. Today it is the ideal return-to-the-past getaway, with pink and white gingerbread trim, and a high ceilinged, golden hued parlor.

Pam and Al lovingly created a romantic atmosphere to share with their guests. In each of the guest rooms they made use of beautiful materials (with many cabbage-rose florals, of course!) and enchantingly eclectic Victorian furniture. The Primrose Pink Room has a free-standing, claw-footed, pink tub beckoning in the corner, with a fluffy robe hanging by its side. And the bright yellow and blue Morning Glory room, with sunlight streaming in through four lace-curtained windows, will convince guests that they are waking up in a field of daisies and buttercups. Every guest room has a complete

china tea set on a table, and guests may arrange to have breakfast brought up to their rooms. Not surprisingly, the Cabbage Rose has become a popular place to celebrate wedding nights and anniversaries.

A baby grand piano, covered with vintage family photographs, dominates the dining room. Weekdays a continental breakfast is served, but on Saturday and Sunday there is a full breakfast that might include an onion/herb or cheese/bacon quiche, stuffed French toast, or pancakes à la Pam's grandmother, with a side of sausage or bacon.

Flemington is a relatively undiscovered area, only sixty miles from both New York City and Philadelphia. The center of town is a National Historical District, surrounded by rural scenery. Flemington does have a reputation for its extensive outlet shopping and over 150 shops (mostly clustered in two Colonial-replica villages) are two blocks from the inn.

THE CABBAGE ROSE INN, 162 Main Street, Flemington, NJ 08822; (908) 788-0247; Pam Venosa and Al Scott, owners. Open all year. Five guest rooms, all with private baths, telephones, air conditioning. Rates: $80 to $120 per room, including full breakfast in room, on porch, or in dining room. No children under 10; no pets; smoking on porch only; Visa/MasterCard/American Express. Extensive and varied outlet shopping in town. Golf, riding, antiquing, auctions, Bucks County browsing, and local wineries.
DIRECTIONS: call.

PENNSYLVANIA

ISAAC STOVER HOUSE

The B&B where Sally Jessy Raphael spared no expense

One of the most opulently eclectic and delightful inns you will ever visit is the Isaac Stover House, a beautifully restored brick Federal-Victorian right on the Delaware River. Originally built by one of the seven Stover brothers, prominent area businessmen, it now belongs to Sally Jessy Raphael, the popular radio and TV talk-show personality.

When she bought the inn in 1987, Sally spared no expense in restoring it to its original Victorian splendor. Guests find themselves greeted by French antiques, Persian carpets, English Chippendale, gilded mirrors, and period paintings. To that, Sally has added her personal treasure trove of collectibles from years of world travel.

A full breakfast is served in the pecan paneled Taproom, with its marble-topped tables. Guests feast on fresh fruit salad, homemade granola and fruit yogurt, homemade breads and muffins. Omelets, home fries, and eggs Benedict constitute the main course.

Hors d'oeuvres are served in the Taproom in the afternoons, and there is a double sitting room and a Greenhouse Room in which guests can relax and mingle.

All of the guest rooms have been recently redone, with bedding coordinated with beautiful wallpapers, carpeting, and accessories.

ISAAC STOVER HOUSE. River Road, P.O. Box 68, Erwinna, PA 18920; (610) 294-8044, Fax (610) 294-8132; Sally Jessy Raphael, owner; Vinny Howe, innkeeper. Open all year. Seven guest rooms, 4 with private baths, 3 semi-private. Rates: $150 to $175, including full breakfast. Children over 12 welcome; no pets; smoking in common rooms only; all credit cards accepted. Hot air balloons pick up at inn. Picnic baskets prepared on request. Fine dining nearby.

DIRECTIONS: from Rte. 78 take Clinton-Pittstown exit 15 and go left onto Rte. 513 south for 11 miles to Frenchtown. Cross bridge to Pennsylvania and go left on Rte. 32 south. Inn is 2 miles on right.

The front entrance.

Luxury prevails in the guest rooms.

THE MANSION INN

A new life for the Grand Old Lady

Almost from the day it was built in 1865, the magnificent manor house set right on the main street of New Hope, Pennsylvania, has attracted admiring glances. It is considered to be a superb example of baroque Victorian architecture.

In recent years its future was in grave doubt, but several businessmen who regularly vacationed in New Hope could see past the deteriorating wood and falling plaster. Instead they envisioned an inn that would recapture the fading elegance of the building. They bought the manor house and began reconstruction. Walls and ceilings were ripped out to create wide open spaces. Six guest rooms were created, many with fireplaces. Antiques and period furniture reproductions were purchased and extensive gardens planted. A new swimming pool and a private parking area were added in back of the inn.

The result is a masterpiece. For example, the inn brochure describes the Buckingham Suite: "A carriage-style suite with queen-sized bed, settee in sitting area, cable television, and a two-person corner Jacuzzi. Pastels of pink, burgundy and olive echo with the garden trellis theme."

Guests staying at the inn can walk to riverfront restaurants, take a ride in a horse-drawn carriage, shop the many stores right outside the inn's front doors, and savor other pleasures of Bucks County.

THE MANSION INN, 9 South Main Street, New Hope, PA 18938; (215) 862-1231; Robert and Nid Stuessy, innkeepers. Seven rooms, all with king or queen beds and private baths. Rates: $165 to $205 per room, including full gourmet breakfast with home-baked breads. Children over 12 welcome; no pets; no smoking; all major credit cards.

DIRECTIONS: on Rte. 32, in the center of New Hope. The Mansion's parking is behind the building on Bridge Street.

Left above, the incredible Victorian craftmanship of the inn building. Below, the guests' library.

Twelve-foot ceilings allow for nobly arched doorways.

More elegantly arched doorways.

THE WHITEHALL INN

A handsome estate in Bucks County

Bucks County is blessed with lush countryside filled with handsome estates that have sheltered generations of landed gentry. And no Bucks County estate is more lovely than the Whitehall Inn. The inn sits secluded on a quiet country byway, yet it is nearby the center of bustling New Hope.

Mike and Suella Wass are the innkeepers *extraordinaire* of this 1795 great house, and their vision of hospitality would exhaust lesser mortals. A day at the Whitehall begins with a leisurely four-course breakfast, prepared by Suella and served by Mike. The Wasses' litany of gourmet breakfast fare is longer than your arm, fit for a four-star restaurant, and striking enough to be featured by *Bon Appetit* magazine. The meal is served on fine European china and crystal, but the real treasure is the Wasses' rare, heirloom sterling, passed down through Suella's family, which is placed, in proper English fashion, top-

Left above, the elegant breakfast table set with heirloom silver.

side-down to reveal the intricacies of the design on the backs.

These energetic innkeepers don't stop here. Mike makes his own bath salts, as well as fragrant rose-scented potpourri, concocted from petals gathered from his prized rose collection; and the Wasses attend to such details as providing each guest room with lead crystal wine glasses and a full bottle of wine produced by a Bucks County vineyard. Each day they prepare a sweet and savory afternoon tea, and they periodically host a theme tea, whose topic pervades the entire weekend. For example: a candlelight tea accompanied by Philadelphia's Fairmount Brass Quartet or by a trio from the New York Philharmonic; a strawberry tea or a chocolate tea, each attended by a speaker knowledgeable on the subject; a romantic champagne-and-candlelight New Year's Eve classical music concert.

THE WHITEHALL INN, RD 2, Box 250, 1370 Pineville Rd., New Hope, PA 18938; (215) 598-7945; Mike and Suella Wass, hosts. Open all year. Six rooms, 4 with private baths, 2 share. Rates: $130 to $190 double, with 4-course candlelight breakfast and afternoon high tea. Children over 12 welcome; no pets; no smoking; all major credit cards accepted. Swimming pool and tennis courts on premises, and dressage horses that accept carrots from guests. All of Bucks County's famous attractions immediately available, including restaurants, menus of which are available.

DIRECTIONS: from New Hope on Rte. 202 south go to traffic light at Street Rd. intersection. Turn left on Street to 2nd intersection at Pineville Rd. Turn right for 1½ miles to inn.

Each of the spacious guest rooms is furnished in a different period.

BUCKSVILLE HOUSE

Hospitality and history combined

At the Bucksville House, history and hospitality go hand-in-hand. The inn is a handsome, creamy stucco house and is the most prominent landmark in the tiny village of Bucksville, which lies a stone's throw from the Delaware River and a short drive to the shops and restaurants that line the streets of New Hope.

In 1795 Captain Nicholas Buck built the original building and founded the village of Bucksville. In 1840, Nicholas Buck, Jr. added more rooms and established a stagecoach-stop hotel to serve travelers journeying between Philadelphia and Easton. Innkeepers Barbara and Joe Szollosi are carrying on this tradition of hospitality, and their inn is a little gem.

Guests feel immediately at home, embraced by the warmth of the surroundings. Throughout the inn Barbara and Joe have carefully recreated the colonial era, with additional contemporary comforts, and the house is spotlessly maintained.

In the morning guests gather around the dining room table to enjoy a full breakfast and to revel in the room's rich colonial ambience. During chilly weather the Szollosis stock the hearth with firewood which adds an extra note of cheer. The breakfast menu might include a casserole of savory eggs or eggs and sausages; bran-raisin-walnut waffles; fresh peach fritters, in season; homemade sticky buns or fruit bread; and assorted fresh fruit and hot beverages.

Guest accommodations range in size from the third-floor suite, which boasts exposed beams and a full sitting room, and the second floor Gold Room, which enjoys one of the inn's original hearths, to the intimate Green Room, which contains a winsome display of vintage toys that were Barbara's childhood playthings.

THE BUCKSVILLE HOUSE, RD 2, Box 146, Rte. 412 and Buck Drive, Kintnersville, PA 18930; (610) 847-8948, Fax (610) 847-8948; Barbara and Joe Szollosi, hosts. Open all year. Four rooms and 1 suite, all with private baths and air conditioning. Rates: from $100 to $130, with full country breakfast and home baking. Children over 12 welcome; no pets; no smoking; all major credit cards, checks accepted. Fishing, canoeing, swimming, riding, tennis, cross-country skiing, antiquing in area, as well as many restaurants.

DIRECTIONS: from Philadelphia take Rte. 611 North through Doylestown for 14 miles to Rte. 412 North. Take left to inn for 2 miles. From New York take Holland Tunnel to Rte. 78 West to Easton, Pa. to Rte. 611 South through Kintnersville for 1 mile to Church Hill Rd. Take right for 1½ miles to Rte. 412. Inn is second house on left.

BRIDGETON HOUSE

French doors onto the Delaware

Bridgeton House sits on the banks of the Delaware River. This is an enviable position, for while many Bucks County hostels advertise proximity to the river as a drawing card, few can truly say the river is their backyard. Beatrice and Charles Briggs restored their seven-room inn with an eye to incorporating the river by installing French doors and laying a pebble patio that sweeps to the edge of the riverbank.

With Charles' talent as a master carpenter and Bea in charge of interior design, the Briggses completely renovated and decorated what was a derelict building, an eyesore caught between the bridge and the road. Today, Bridgeton House feels like a cross between American country-naive and French provincial style. Bea uses soft color throughout, Williamsburg shades of faded cobalt, muted mulberry, and clotted cream. Thick rag rugs and a collection of antique Oriental area rugs accent painted hardwood floors. Fine bed linens and puffy comforters please the eye and assure the traveler of a comfortable night's sleep.

Bridgeton House is a casual, but sophisticated environment. Before becoming innkeepers, Bea and Charles worked in Bucks County inns and restaurants, and their years of experience show. Always available, but never intrusive, Bea sets a relaxing tone. She loves to cook and often can be found in the inn's beautiful kitchen, which opens onto the entry hall and adjoining dining room.

Outside the door, the Delaware River affords many diversions, starting with its lovely sixty-mile towpath, which is perfect for hiking, cross-country skiing, picnicking, and jogging. Canoeing, fishing, and tubing enthusiasts proclaim the Delaware to be among the East Coast's finest rivers.

BRIDGETON HOUSE, River Rd., Upper Black Eddy, PA 18972; (610) 982-5856; Charles and Beatrice Briggs, proprietors. Built in 1836 as a private residence, this home also once served as a bakery and candy store. Open year-round. Seven guest rooms, two suites, one penthouse, some with river views and balconies, all with private baths. Rates: on weekends by room $79–$199. Full breakfast. Good restaurants close by. Children discouraged on weekends; no pets; no smoking; Visa/MasterCard, personal checks accepted.

DIRECTIONS: from Philadelphia, take I-95 north to New Hope/Yardley exit. Follow signs north to New Hope. Continue north on Rte. 32, 18 miles to inn.

The elegant entry hall.

THE INN AT FORDHOOK FARM

Burpee seeds branches out

The Inn at Fordhook Farm stands as a monument to quiet, old world elegance. Three generations of the Burpee family, purveyors of world-class seeds, entertained guests in this charming, predominantly eighteenth-century fieldstone residence. The tradition is continuing since Blanche Burpee Dohan and Jonathan Burpee, the firm's founder's grandchildren, opened the house as an eminently comfortable bed and breakfast.

Each of the five rooms, named for different family members, has its own appeal, although honeymoon couples tend to gravitate to the spacious Burpee Room with its colonial revival fireplace and private balcony or to the stately Atlee Room, accented with leaded glass windows, fireplace, and balcony. The smaller Curtiss Room is a cozy nook with slanted roof and gorgeous view of the grounds. Double pocket doors distinguish the Torrance Room, as sunshine, peach hues, and three mirrored closet panels enhance the Simmons Room. The linden tree outside is a "a favorite haunt of the hoot owl," says Blanche.

Trees form an outstanding backdrop here along with the numerous gardens, including former seed-trial beds. Daffodils carpet the lawn's edge in spring, while marigolds last until the first frost. Lilacs, wisteria, and perennials dot the grounds amid gingkos, sycamores, dogwood, magnolia, rhododendrons and azalea, all befitting the gracious home of one of the most famous men in seed history.

THE INN AT FORDHOOK FARM, 105 New Britain Rd., Doylestown, PA 18901; (215) 345-1766, Fax (215) 345-1791; Carole Burpee and Janice Webb, innkeepers. Open all year. Five guest rooms, 3 with private baths, 2 with fireplaces; suite arrangement available. Rates: $95 to $150; additional person, $20; 2-bedroom carriage house from $175 to $300. Full farm breakfast included; afternoon tea served on the terrace. Children over 12 welcome; no pets; smoking on the terrace only; Visa/MasterCard/American Express. Tubing, canoeing, rafting, swimming, tennis, horseback riding, ice skating, cross-country skiing nearby; Mercer Museum and Moravian Tile Works; antiquing. Excellent dining in the area.

DIRECTIONS: The Inn at Fordhook Farm is located at Rte. 202 and the 611 bypass, 1.6 miles west of Doylestown. From Doylestown follow Rte. 202 south past the hospital and over the 611 bypass. Turn left on New Britain Rd. (first road on your left next to Delaware Valley College). The entrance to Fordhook is ¼ mile on your left through two stone pillars. Follow the drive over the little bridge to the large stone house on the right.

Above, the Breakfast Room.

Oscar Hammerstein's personal estate, where he wrote many famous songs.

HIGHLAND FARMS

Memories of Oscar

Oscar Hammerstein, the renowned lyricist of *Oh What A Beautiful Morning* penned that song along with many of his other hits while sitting on the porch of this inn when it was his personal estate. The eighteenth-century stately gray-stucco home is now a distinctive bed and breakfast, filled with its own unique history.

Memories of Oscar Hammerstein are everywhere. Each of the four guest rooms is named for a musical, and playbills and sheet music are part of their décor. There is a comfortable video library where guests may view tapes of his shows. *The Sound of Music* is written on the floor of the sixty-foot, pear-shaped swimming pool (Why pear-shaped? Because it was Mr. Hammerstein's favorite fruit, of course!). And the sound of *his* music accompanies breakfast, served with antique silverware in the former music room.

Breakfast is a sumptuous four-course event, served on the outdoor patio in warm weather. A special afternoon treat is presented daily between 5 and 6 o'clock: a pitcher of Highland Farms drinks (a creamy, citrusy wine punch) along with homemade crackers or hot roasted nuts. Served poolside, weather permitting, it is a perfect transition into evening on this peaceful countryside estate.

Mary Schnitzer's talents are not limited to her marvelous hospitality and cooking. Her handpainted motifs are in many of the rooms, including a horse on the wall of the Carousel Room.

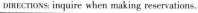

HIGHLAND FARMS, 70 East Road, Doylestown, PA 18901; (215) 340-1354; Mary Schnitzer, owner. Open all year. Four rooms, 2 with private baths and 2 semi-private. Rates: $125 to $175 double, including full, 4-course breakfast, special afternoon treats, and sherry in the evening. Children over 12 welcome; no pets; smoking in library only; Visa/MasterCard/American Express. Swimming pool and tennis courts on property. Wonderful dining in area.

DIRECTIONS: inquire when making reservations.

PINE TREE FARM

An elegant country estate

If you are looking for a tranquil country weekend, that is exactly what you will find at the end of the oak-shaded lane that leads to Pine Tree Farm. Built of native fieldstone in 1730 by a Quaker farmer, it was one of the first homes in the area. Today, the farm is an elegant country estate situated on sixteen-acres of rustic Bucks County.

Owners Joy and Ron Feigles share the entire first floor of their wonderful home with guests. The solarium offers relaxation country style, with a stunning view of woods and pond. A terrace and a swimming pool and tennis court are just outside in the garden.

Rooms are furnished with colors and fabrics reminiscent of the eighteenth-century proprietors of the farm, but with all the amenities of twentieth-century life. One of the four guest rooms has a spectacular white-twig canopied bed. Ron's collection of carved duck decoys is displayed throughout the house and, says Joy, "We've had more than one guest become a collector after staying here."

As life-long residents of the area (in fact, Joy's family came over on the good ship *Welcome* with

Joy Feigles welcomes you.

William Penn!) your hosts are happy to share their knowledge and recommendations with guests. Nearby Doylestown offers fine dining, shopping, and art, as well as the unique Mercer Museums. Henry Mercer, a local gentleman-doctor, dedicated his life to a collection of early American tools, from adzes to zithers, now housed in a concrete castle.

PINE TREE FARM, 2155 Lower State Road, Doylestown, PA 18901; (215) 348-0632; Ron and Joy Feigles, owners. Open all year. Four guest rooms with queen beds and private baths; 2-bedroom suite available. Rates: $135 to $165 per room, including full breakfast at private tables. Open pantry for soda, ice, cookies. No children; no pets; no smoking; no credit cards. Farm has its own swimming pool. Outstanding restaurants nearby.

DIRECTIONS: take Rte. 202 south through the center of Doylestown to 2nd traffic light. Bear left on to Court Street for 1 mile.

Indoor-outdoor living.

BARLEY SHEAF FARM

Charm and romance for blithe spirits

A sense that all's right with the world is the hallmark of the best inns. Barley Sheaf Farm in Bucks County emanates that wonderful feeling of security and comfort.

The property has attracted blithe and sophisticated spirits throughout its life, most notably when it was owned by playwright George S. Kaufman, and weekend guests included Moss Hart, Lillian Hellman, S.J. Perlman, and Alexander Woollcott.

Today, Peter and Veronika Suess's guests may stay in the farmhouse or in one of three bedrooms in the converted ice house. Bedrooms in the main house vary in size, but total charm is assured in each. A two-room suite furnished with an impressive brass sleigh bed, broad and comfortable upholstered couch, working fireplace, and French doors with handpainted privacy screen is the largest bedchamber. The separate ice house, comprising a living room with three very individual, country-style bedrooms, is tailor-made for couples traveling together.

A great percentage of the foodstuffs for a truly splendid three-course breakfast come from the farm; the innkeepers keep bees and harvest a large crop of raspberries each year. A scrumptious main course might be fresh farm eggs scrambled and served with salmon, a sweet pepper and onion frittata, or ham or sausage, complemented with a variety of fragrant, homebaked Swiss breads, homemade jams, and genuine farm honey. And there is always a pot of freshly brewed coffee ready and waiting.

BARLEY SHEAF FARM, Box 10, Rte. 202, Holicong, PA 18928; (215) 794-5104; Pete and Veronika Suess, owners. Open all year except Christmas week. Seven guest rooms in main house, plus three in cottage; private baths. Rates: $130 to $195. $20 per extra person; single $15 less. Full breakfast served. Wide selection of restaurants in area. No children under eight; no pets; French and German spoken. Visa/MasterCard/American Express, checks accepted.

DIRECTIONS: from Philadelphia, take I-95 north to exit 332 (Newtown). Turn left at exit and drive to fifth light, turning right onto Rte. 532. Take first left at Goodnoes Restaurant and then turn right onto Rte. 413 north. Follow 413 for about twelve minutes and turn right at intersection of Rte. 202. Farm is on the right about a five-minute drive on 202.

LA RESERVE

A B&B with a French flavor

Built in the 1850's, this four-story townhouse has survived and prospered. Meticulously maintained as a city residence for more than 130 years, it has latterly become a haven for travelers, many from Europe—particularly France.

The parlor is elegant. A candelabra-lit Steinway grand piano of rare vintage awaits your touch. Nearby is a lavishly gilded pier mirror offset by tall silk-draped windows. There are two blue-tufted settees, smartly covered side chairs, and an opulently gilded fireplace, strikingly fanciful, a surprising departure from the staid exterior.

Seven spacious guest rooms, including two generously proportioned suites, have sitting areas, decorative fireplaces, some with bookcases and desks. Three have private baths.

A full breakfast is served in the bay-windowed formal dining room. Offerings vary daily, but always include an egg dish. There is a lovely flower garden to retire to with a cup of fragrant coffee and the morning paper.

Two blocks from elegant Rittenhouse Square, the inn is just steps away from the Civil War Library and the Rosenbach Museum and Library.

LA RESERVE, 1804 Pine Street, Philadelphia, PA 19103; (800) 354-8401, (215) 735-1137 or 0582; Bill Buchanan, manager. Open all year. Eight rooms, 3 with private baths, 5 sharing; all rooms air conditioned. Rates: $45 to $85 per room, including full breakfast. Children welcome; pets on occasion; no smoking preferred; Visa/MasterCard. In Rittenhouse Square area, with lots of first-class restaurants. Pretty garden invites lingering.

DIRECTIONS: south of Rittenhouse Square.

One of the guest rooms.

The sitting room.

THE THOMAS BOND HOUSE

A historical gem

Most Philadelphia buildings are rife with history, and the Thomas Bond House is no exception. Built in 1769 by a physician and surgeon who, with Benjamin Franklin, founded the first public hospital in America, the house is an important example of the Georgian Classic Revival style of colonial architecture.

Serving as a residence until 1810, the house subsequently had quite a history, functioning as a stocking manufactory, leather tannery, customs brokerage house, and a retail shop, until restored by the National Park Service as a bed and breakfast residence in 1988.

Carefully restored and furnished in the Federal Period, the twelve guest rooms vary from suites on the first floor with queen-sized beds, working fireplaces, and whirlpool baths to two smaller, more simple rooms set in the top-floor pediment.

Weekdays, breakfast is continental, with orange juice and freshly baked muffins. On weekends, however, guests are treated to a sumptuous full breakfast in the formal dining room

Evenings start with complimentary wine and cheese in front of the working fireplace in the charmingly decorated parlor. Afterwards, the innkeeper will cheerfully make dinner reservations for guests at any of the many excellent restaurants in the area.

A guest room.

THE THOMAS BOND HOUSE, 129 South 2nd Street, Philadelphia, PA 19106; (800) 845-BOND; Thomas Lantry, managing partner, George Phillips, innkeeper. Open all year. Twelve guest rooms, including 2 suites, all with private baths. Rates: $90 to $160 per room or suite, including continental breakfast on weekdays and full breakfast on weekends. Wine and cheese is served in the evenings before dinner hour. Children welcome; no pets; no smoking; Visa/MasterCard/ Diners. On the grounds of Independence National Historic Park with the Liberty Bell, Independence Hall, Congress Hall, U.S. Mint, Betsy Ross house; menus available.

DIRECTIONS: downtown Philadelphia near Independence Hall.

A guest room.

SHIPPEN WAY INN

A trio of landmark houses

The Shippen Way Inn is one of Philadelphia's most charming bed and breakfasts. It consists of three landmark houses joined together.

Conveniently linked to the past—near Penn's Landing, Independence Hall, and Benjamin Franklin's Printing Shop—it also borders on South Street, a village within the city, overflowing with trendy restaurants, cafés, galleries, and boutiques.

Nine individually appointed guest rooms include: The Cotswold Room, reminiscent of an English garden; The Blue Room, with a stained-glass window and papered in Laura Ashley; The Quilt Room, furnished in colonial style with handwoven fabrics and quilts; The Rose Room, with a private entrance off the colonial herb and rose garden; and The Four Poster room with a bed so high it requires the use of bed steps.

An elaborate continental breakfast includes home baked breads and fresh fruits. Tea or wine and cheese are served in the afternoon.

A spinning wheel, a cobbler's bench, and other colonial objects are artfully placed throughout. The living room has a fireplace for cozy winter evenings. Carriage rides can be arranged for doing the city in style.

SHIPPEN WAY INN, 416–18 Bainbridge Street, Philadelphia, PA 19147; (800) 245-4873; (215) 627-7266; Ann Foringer and Raymond Rhule, owners. Open all year. Nine rooms with private baths. Rates: $70 to $105 per room, including continental breakfast and afternoon refreshments. Inquire about children; no pets; smoking in garden; all major credit cards. Many restaurants nearby on South Street 1 block away.

DIRECTIONS: very near Independence Park, with its historic buildings.

VALLEY FORGE

An ageless colonial beauty

This large stone colonial is an ageless beauty of the pre-Revolutionary period. Nestled on four acres of magnificently wooded land, its title deeds can be traced back to William Penn in 1681.

The original part of the house was built before 1720. Two additions built later create the overall traditional colonial appearance. The last addition was completed in 1791.

Over the years, interior walls have been added and removed, but the original random width plank flooring, with hand-forged nails, remains. The old wood floors, fireplaces, stone walls, and stone smoke house were there when George Washington was at Valley Forge.

A highlight of a stay here is the full English-style breakfast, graciously served in the old part of the house in front of the colonial fireplace with a huge mantel and eight-foot-wide hearth.

Two guest rooms occupy the entire third floor, providing spacious privacy for couples or families. The rose and grey room has a canopied queen-sized bed. The second chamber exudes a fresh "peaches and cream" Victorian look and has an antique double brass bed and a twin bed.

VALLEY FORGE. Open all year. Three guest rooms, one with private bath, 2 sharing. Rates: $70 to $80; $10 less for single; includes hearty full gourmet breakfast. Children welcome (cradle and crib available); no pets; smoking outside; heated pool. Philadelphia 18 miles. *Represented by Assn. of Bed & Breakfasts in Philadelphia, Valley Forge, Brandywine; reservations (800) 344-0123, (610) 783-7838, Fax (610) 783-7783.*

Breakfast is served in the pre-1720 part of the house.

HARRY PACKER MANSION

A spectacular wedding present

The age of elegance produced some of the most spectacular architecture of all time. The Harry Packer Mansion is no exception. "An architect used this house as his inspiration for the Haunted Mansion in Walt Disney World," remarked Patricia Handwerk, who, with her husband Bob, is painstakingly restoring the house, keeping the old ceiling paintings, gilt cove work, and other particulars intact wherever possible.

Many of the elaborate, ornate extravagances that characterize the house can be attributed to Asa Packer, the founder of the Lehigh Valley Railroad, who presented the mansion to his son as a wedding present in 1874. From the very outside the noble details begin. Minton tile paves the floor of the Corinthian-columned veranda. The main entrance's 450-pound, etched-glass paneled doors open onto oak parquet floors. The Reception Room, the only common area not furnished according to Packer's plan, sports a walnut mantel and red pine floors. The adjoining library boasts an intricately sculpted mantel of sixteenth-century Caen stone that came from a British manor house. Above the fireplace rests a handsome niche of rich mahogany that follows through into dark paneled walls and a solid-beamed ceiling with oak inserts. The bathroom off the library retains the original mahogany toilet seat, a delicate Limoges basin set in a pink marble sink highlighted by silver spigots. The effect is entrancing.

THE HARRY PACKER MANSION, Packer Hill, Jim Thorpe, PA 18229; (717) 325-8566; Robert and Pat Handwerk, hosts. Open year round. Second Empire stone-and-brick mansion with cast iron trim. Seven spacious guest rooms, four with private baths. Rates: $75 to $130; carriage house with four rooms with private baths, $85 to $95; includes a full, elegant breakfast in the dining room. Children weekdays only; no pets; smoking in common rooms only. MasterCard/Visa/American Express. Steam train on summer weekends; mule and horseback riding; whitewater canoeing; Lake Mauch Chunk nearby; mountain biking. Call for details concerning Mystery Weekends, balls, and other special events.

DIRECTIONS: from the Pennsylvania Turnpike Northeast Extension, take exit 34. Continue 6 miles south on Rte. 209. Follow signs up the hill to the mansion.

The imposing inn building sits on a corner lot across the street from Centre Park.

INN AT CENTRE PARK

Furnished with exquisite taste

Perched in the heart of Reading's historic district is one of the most beautiful bed and breakfast inns you will ever visit. Carefully restored by charming hometown owners Michael and Andrea Smith, it presents an ambience that is at once elegant, gracious, and highly romantic. From the house's embellished gothic façade and porches, to the frieze of playful cherubs that border the ceiling in the grand music room, to the William Morris style Victorian wallpaper in the majestic center hall, to the paneling and wainscoting in most of the rooms, the eye lingers lovingly on every detail.

Awash in a sea of muted greens and ivory is the Green Room Suite, furnished with antique French oak pieces. Capped off by ornamental stained glass, an archway frames the divide between bedchamber and sitting room.

The Governor's Suite's king-size bed, a reproduc-

Left above, the parlor, showing the uniquely decorative baroque plasterwork. Below left, a garden of stained glass separates the Green Room's bedroom from its sitting room. Below right, The Master Suite bedroom.

tion of a French provincial sleigh bed, looks out on the focal point of the suite, the colossal red marble fireplace. The suite's handsomely paneled study was assembled from the burnished chestnut paneling removed from an Austrian château and fitted in flawlessly.

Finally, the Peach Room, accented in black and peach paisley, has a black iron four-poster queen-size bed draped in gauzy white fabric. Its bathroom boasts Reading's first shower.

Breakfast is served in the romantic solarium with innkeeper Andrea serving up such tasty creations as tropical pancakes and peach-stuffed French toast.

To cap off your visit here, try the Thursday, Friday, or Saturday evening dinners or the Sunday brunch. Served in these elegant surroundings you can eat the "best steak in town" or perhaps a rack of lamb, veal chop, fresh fish, or creative vegetarian offerings deliciously prepared by the owner-chef.

THE INN AT CENTRE PARK, 730 Centre Avenue, Reading, PA 19601; (800) 447-1094, (610) 374-8557, Fax (610) 374-8725; Michael and Andrea Smith, owners. Open all year. One room and two suites with fireplaces, all with baths and air conditioning. Rates: $130 to $190 (weekends), $120 to $175 (weekdays), including full breakfast ranging from homemade organic museli to tropical pancakes to peach-stuffed French toast. Inquire about children; no pets; no smoking; Visa/MasterCard. Recommended for dining: Greenhills, Piceno's, and Joe's, famous throughout America for its mushroom specialties. Reading leads the world in outlet shopping and the environs lead in antiquing.

DIRECTIONS: call for directions from downtown Reading.

The Washington Room.

The Princess Room.

CLEARVIEW FARM B&B

In love with farm living

When many people think of the Pennsylvania Dutch country they think of rolling countryside and picture-perfect farms and farmland. They can live within this picture by staying at Clearview Farm Bed & Breakfast.

The limestone farmhouse, built in 1814, serves as the centerpiece of your stay. It overlooks a large pond graced by several white swans and is surrounded by a colorful, well-kept lawn on 200 acres of peaceful farmland. There's an outdoor seating area that's simply hard to resist. It's difficult to stay inside in this environment, but it's easier once you step through the front door.

Owners Glenn and Mildred Wissler have lived on the farm for more than thirty years and have created a unique mix of country style and Victorian charm. All of the guest rooms are tastefully furnished with local antiques (Mildred's father was an antiques dealer and can offer local shopping tips). All offer comfortable sitting areas amidst the antiques. Three of the rooms feature canopied beds, while a fourth offers a carved walnut Victorian bed, and the fifth has an antique iron and brass bed. Room highlights include a dry sink, farm tables, a Victorian marble-top dresser and wash stand, and a claw foot tub.

Mildred prepares a full country breakfast each morning and serves it in their formal dining room. It's a setting perfect for a gentleman farmer.

Left, swans grace the lake in front of the farmhouse.

A bathroom fit for a princess.

CLEARVIEW FARM BED & BREAKFAST, 355 Clearview Road, Ephrata, PA 17522; (717) 733-6333; Glenn and Mildred Wissler, owners and innkeepers. Open all year. Five guest rooms, four with queen beds, one with a double bed, and all with private baths (three with showers and two with showers and tubs). Rates: $95 to $130, including a full breakfast. No pets; major credit cards; smoking outdoors. Lots of country-style dining in area. Near lots of recreational and sightseeing opportunities, including hiking, biking, antiques shopping, and the Pennsylvania Dutch countryside. AAA Four Diamond Award.

DIRECTIONS: from Lancaster, take Rte. 272 north to US-322 west. Follow US-322 west for four miles and take a right on Clearview Road. Take this road about one mile to the first property on the right.

Werner and Debrah Mosimann, owners.

SWISS WOODS B&B

A Swiss haven in Pennsylvania

Werner and Debbie Mosimann set out to create a natural Swiss wonderland in Pennsylvania Dutch country and they have a colorful success on their hands. Lancaster County native Debbie met Switzerland native Werner while both were in Europe. They married, lived there for five years, then moved to Lancaster County to build their home on land that's been in her family for twelve generations.

Set on thirty wooded acres overlooking Speedwell Lake north of the quaint town of Lititz, Swiss Woods Bed & Breakfast features seven modern European-style rooms with names like Lake of Geneva, Appenzell, The Matterhorn, and Wilhelm Tell. The Anker Stube (common room) is dominated by a massive sandstone fireplace and provides the heartbeat for the inn's activities. Debbie serves huge breakfasts in this room, including soufflés, French toast, and Berchermuesli (a Swiss fruit and yogurt dish).

But the soul of Swiss Woods is outside, where Werner's special talent is evidenced with the profu-

Left, the garden setting of the inn.

Breakfast al fresco.

sion of flowers surrounding the inn. Annuals, unusual perennials, flowering shrubs, and bushes abound. Woodland wildflowers, like the illusive Jack-in-the-Pulpit, peek out from the edges of paths. Bee Balm attracts the birds, buddleia draws the butterflies, and nature lovers bring out binoculars provided by the inn. It's a wild and wonderful experience.

SWISS WOODS BED & BREAKFAST. 500 Blantz Road, Lititz, PA 17543; (717) 627-3358 or (800) 594-8018; FAX (717) 627-3483; Werner and Debrah Mosimann, owners and innkeepers. Open all year (except Dec. 24 to Dec. 26). Seven guest rooms, all with queen beds and private baths (2 with whirlpool tubs). Rates: $70 to $105 single, $85 to $130 double, including a full breakfast. Children welcome; no pets; major credit cards; smoking outdoors; German and Swiss German spoken. Lots of country-style dining in area. Near lots of recreational and sightseeing opportunities, including hiking, canoeing on the nearby lake, biking, birding.

DIRECTIONS: from Lancaster, take 501 north through Lititz. Turn left onto Brubaker Valley Road and go one mile to the lake. Before crossing the lake, turn right onto Blantz Road. Swiss Woods is the first lane on the left.

The rustic sitting room.

The balcony of this guest room can be seen on the front of the inn in the photo opposite.

Handmade beds and quilts in the guest rooms.

SMITHTON

Pennsylvania Dutch hospitality

In the mid-1700s Henry and Susana Miller were devout members of the Ephrata Community, a Protestant monastic religious group founded by charismatic leader Johann Conrad Beissel. As "outdoor members," the Millers lived by a more relaxed discipline than the majority of disciples, who were celibate and ascetic. The Millers' home, a sturdy stone structure that served as a tavern and stagecoach stop, sat on a hill overlooking the Community Cloister. The Cloister was a remarkably beautiful group of medieval German buildings constructed along the banks of the Cocalico Creek, where Beissel and his followers lived and worked. Although the community of believers declined over the years, the Cloister remains—as does the Millers' home, which is now an inn called Smithton.

Smithton is a warm and welcoming home, and Dorothy Graybill, a Lancaster County native, is the gracious hostess. In this inn guests are steeped in two centuries of history while treated to the the true spirit of Pennsylvania Dutch hospitality. Throughout the house, from the airy kitchen and adjoining dining room to the deluxe, two-story suite complete with whirlpool tub, they will enjoy the special attention that is given to wood, from handmade beds and Windsor chairs to hand-fashioned latches and hinges, their design taken from a Cloister pattern. The focal point of each bedroom is the traditional bright and cheerful, handstitched quilt—made by one of the local Pennsylvania Dutch ladies, of course. Extra-large, square down pillows, perfect props for a good read in bed, and soft flannel nightshirts hanging behind each door are just two of many thoughtful and creative touches.

SMITHTON. 900 W. Main St., Ephrata, PA 17522; (717) 733-6094; Dorothy Graybill, hostess. Rustic stone house built in 1763. Seven guest rooms plus one suite, all with private baths. Modest extra charge for third person. Open year-round. Rates: $65 to $150 rooms, $140 to $170 for suite, third person extra (no fee for infants). Full breakfast. Interesting choice of restaurants in area. Well-mannered children and pets accepted only by previous arrangement; major credit cards and checks; must prepay in full.

DIRECTIONS: from north or south, take Rte. 222 to the Ephrata exit. Turn west on Rte. 322 (Ephrata's Main Street) and drive 2½ miles to Smithton.

THE CHURCHTOWN INN

Special innkeepers

The Churchtown Inn, a splendid fieldstone mansion, is the most prominent landmark in this tiny village overlooking the pastoral, picture-postcard fields and farms of the Pennsylvania Dutch countryside. Built in 1735, the house was owned by prominent Pennsylvanian Edward Davies, a member of the 25th Congress and a state legislator from 1804 to 1853. Today, innkeepers Hermine and Stuart Smith and Jim Kent have furnished the house with personal treasures and warm spirits, making for a very relaxed and comfortable inn.

The Smiths' previous life—he was director of the Stuart W. Smith Singers, which performed in such prestigious houses as Carnegie Hall and Lincoln Center—offered opportunity to globetrot, and this rambling, three-story inn is filled with antiques, *objets d'art*, collectibles, and conversa-

tion pieces. In the first-floor parlors you'll find French, English, and American antique furniture, Italian woodcarvings, a Regina music box, and Stuart's grand piano. Guest bedrooms are tucked here and there on the second and third floors; antique bedsteads and Amish quilts are the focus of each chamber. A marvelous new glass breakfast room overlooks the Welsh Mountains.

Each Saturday evening guests are offered the rare opportunity to adjourn to a local Amish family's farm to enjoy a bountiful dinner, during which they may be serenaded by the family's daughters, who excel at harmonious religious hymns. Afterward, back at the inn, Stuart often regales his guests with a short piano concert.

THE CHURCHTOWN INN BED & BREAKFAST. Rte. 23, Churchtown, PA 17555; mail to P.O. Box 135, RD 3, Narvon, PA 17555; (215) 445-7794; Hermine and Stuart Smith, hosts. Open all year. Eight rooms, including a carriage house, all with private baths. Rates: $65 to $125 double, with full 5-course breakfast. Children over 12 welcome; no pets; smoking outside; Visa/MasterCard; limited German and Italian spoken. Special events weekends, including Thanksgiving and Christmas, from Nov. 15 to May 30. Area dining includes Pennsylvania Dutch smorgasbord.

DIRECTIONS: going west on Pennsylvania Turnpike take exit 22 (Morgantown) to 23 West for 3 miles to inn. From south take I-83 north to Rte. 30 east to Rte. 23 east.

The warm and elegant front foyer.

Maison
Rouge
bed and breakfast
2236 Marietta Ave.
399-3033

The Senator's Room, with its four-poster cannonball bed.

MAISON ROUGE B&B

An elegant Victorian getaway

For Rod Petrocci and Bill Stomski, Victorian elegance is in the details. From the formal dining room to designer wallcoverings, the details add up to make this bed and breakfast an elegant Victorian getaway near centrally located Lancaster.

From the moment you step inside this Second Empire Victorian home, you are enveloped in exquisitely decorated rooms that take hours to fully explore and enjoy. The formal parlor, library, and game room are filled with antiques, and any one is a perfect place for relaxation or afternoon tea.

Upstairs, the large guest rooms feature many little touches that Rod and Bill can lovingly explain. If you feel like you're in an English country garden, it's because Maison Rouge was chosen for a photo spread to introduce a new line of wallcoverings and fabrics produced by Hanover-based Eisenhart Wallcoverings. Known as the Kilburn Collection, it was

Left, a Second Empire Victorian gem built in 1882.

The co-owner, Rod Petrocci.

inspired by the works of eighteenth-century English artist William Kilburn, who created a wide range of botanical designs as renderings for textiles. The results are stunning guest rooms for all to enjoy. A manicured garden is at the back of the house, with seasonal offerings like azaleas, tulips, chrysanthemums, daffodils, and others that are picked and placed in the guest rooms and on the dining room table.

In the morning, a four-course gourmet breakfast is served in their formal dining room, using fine antique china and crystal. Chilled strawberry soup, stuffed French toast, smoked bacon or sausage, pumpkin custard, or poached pears are some of the treats in store. It's a perfect time to savor the details of this room and the other little touches of elegance throughout Maison Rouge.

MAISON ROUGE BED AND BREAKFAST: 2236 Marietta Avenue, P.O. Box 6243, Lancaster, PA 17607; (717) 399-3033 or (800) 309-3033; Rodney J. Petrocci and William L. Stomski, owners and innkeepers. Open all year. Four guest rooms, all with queen beds, sitting areas, and private baths. Rates: $80 to $120 per room, including a full breakfast. Children over 12 welcome; no pets; major credit cards; smoking outdoors. Lots of country-style dining in area. Near lots of recreational and sightseeing opportunities, including a wide range of possibilities in Lancaster and the surrounding Pennsylvania Dutch countryside.

DIRECTIONS: from Rte. 30 or Rte. 283, take the Rte. 741 exit and travel east to Marietta Avenue (Rte. 23) and turn right. Maison Rouge is located just two blocks after this turn, on the corner of Elizabeth Street and Marietta Avenue.

Right, a table set with a Russian tea service.

A table setting of Wedgewood Countryside china. The decorative cherubs are Italian.

The Empire Room.

Well worth the visit, winter or summer.

THE HAWK MOUNTAIN INN

Paradise for bird watchers

With stunning views overlooking the foothills of the Blue Mountain Valley, Hawk Mountain Inn offers the nearest lodging to one of America's foremost bird watching sites. Hawk Mountain Sanctuary is a 2,200 acre wildlife refuge where bald eagles, ospreys, broad-winged hawks, and other rare species have soared for centuries. Nature lovers and ornithologists from around the world, who observe these beautiful creatures, now have wonderful lodgings that blend the finest European bed and breakfast traditions with the American accent on comfort and luxury.

Built in 1988 by Jim and Judy Gaffney, the inn has eight guest rooms, each one uniquely furnished with eclectic post-Victorian pieces, including rice, pencil post, and pineapple bedsteads, matching comforters, carpeting, window accents, and armoires incorporating TV units.

A Common Room dominated by a large native stone fireplace has a bar and a library of classic books. Here is where sumptuous breakfasts are served, and offerings may include fresh eggs, pork roll, slab bacon, whole wheat pancakes, omelets, or waffles.

Local activities vary with the seasons, and in addition to bird watching, there is hiking on nearby Appalachian trails, county fairs, skiing, antiquing, steam locomotive rides, shopping at Reading's famous factory outlets, and dining at the area's fine restaurants—all in the heart of Pennsylvania Dutch country.

THE HAWK MOUNTAIN INN. Rd 1, Box 186, Stony Run Valley Road, Kempton, PA 19529; (610) 756-4224; Jim and Judy Gaffney, owners. Open all year. Eight rooms with private baths, 2 with Jacuzzis, 2 with fireplaces. Rates: $65 to $95 single, $95 to $135 double; includes full breakfast and complimentary beer and soda on tap. Children welcome; inquire about pets; smoking allowed; French and German spoken; Visa/MasterCard/American Express. Dining room on premises open Thurs. to Sat.; Pennsylvania Dutch cooking in area. Birdwatching, skiing, antiquing, shopping at outlet stores.

DIRECTIONS: from east, exit from Rte. 78/22 northward onto Rte. 737 and proceed 2½ miles to left turn and follow road 1 mile to inn.

Ray Constance Hearne making breakfast.

SPRING HOUSE

"Back to basics"

Ray Constance Hearne, a gracious and wise hostess, restored this 1798 historic house with a deliberateness guided by a preservationist's philosophy: "Buildings should show their age and reflect their history". When Ray mentions "back to basics," she means antiques, feather beds, down puffs, flannel sheets, and wholesome foods. "I get eggs from chickens that run around outside and eat grass." A weekend here, riding horseback across the swales, matched with a trip to the nearby Allegro Vineyards and one of the locale's fine restaurants combines for an excellent cure for frazzled nerves.

SPRING HOUSE, Muddy Creek Forks, York County, Airville, PA 17302; (717) 927-6906; Ray Constance Hearne, innkeeper. Open year round. Spanish and French spoken. Four guest rooms, two with private baths. Rates: $60 to $85, including a hearty breakfast. Refreshment served on arrival. Children welcome; pets boarded nearby (reservations recommended); no smoking; no credit cards.

DIRECTIONS: from the east take Rte. 202 to the Pennsylvania Turnpike. Pick up Rte. 202 again at King of Prussia (exit Rte. 30 west) and take the Rte. 30 bypass. Go south on 41 to Atglen, 372 west across the Susquehanna, and a right onto 74 north. At Brogue, turn left at the post office. Muddy Creek Forks is 5 miles; at the bottom of the hill is Spring House.

MAPLE LANE

In the heart of Amish country

It's Marion Rohrer's touch that makes Maple Lane so special; she adds a homespun air to an otherwise modern colonial home. Pierced parchment lampshades glow into the evenings, when guests curl up in one of Marion's or her daughter-in-law's quilts. Similar coverlets are offered for sale in a nook on the first floor. If the Rohrer family offerings don't fit the bill, Marion kindly directs serious buyers to neighboring Amish farms.

Longtime residents of Paradise, the Rohrers own and operate a working dairy farm with about two hundred head of cows. Ed welcomes guests to watch the milking, and he invites children to help feed the calves. Guests and grandchildren are the Rohrer's hobbies, so Ed loves to answer questions about the farm while Marion keeps track of all the auctions, farmers' markets, and antiques shops.

This is the heart of Amish country. Although Maple Lane is not an Amish farm—three of its neighbors are—the Rohrers maintain a refreshing air of simplicity and kindness.

MAPLE LANE GUEST HOUSE, 505 Paradise Lane, Paradise, PA 17562; (717) 687-7479. Ed and Marion Rohrer, hosts. Open year-round. Four guests rooms with two baths. Modern two-story colonial within sight of a 1785 stone house and Amish farms. Rates: $50 to $60. Includes continental breakfast. Children welcome; no pets; smokers encouraged to use the outside porch in warm weather. Two-night minimum on weekends. Tourist attractions, shopping, antiquing, historic homes nearby. Pennsylvania Dutch restaurants in abundance.

DIRECTIONS: turn south on Rte. 896 from Rte. 30. Proceed to Strasbourg; turn left on Rte. 896 at the traffic light and continue 1½ miles out of town. Turn right at the sign for the Timberline Lodge. Maple Lane is the first farm on the left.

The Diller Suite.

BEECHMONT INN

Breakfast is one of the highlights

Beechmont is a handsome Georgian townhouse, set a few blocks from Hanover's town square and just twenty miles east of historic Gettysburg. Built in 1834, when Andrew Jackson was president, the inn witnessed several major Civil War clashes, first when General Kilpatrick confronted Jeb Stuart and was forced to retreat down the avenue in front of the inn, and again when General George Custer pushed the Confederates back down through the center of Hanover.

Innkeepers William and Susan Day furnished their inn with a collection of antiques from the Federal period, befitting the age of the house, as well as a blend of assorted, comfortable period pieces. Two of the inn's three guest suites are located on the first floor. The amply proportioned Diller Suite, with a queen-size canopied bed, working fireplace, and whirlpool tub, is ideal for guests who choose to linger in the area. The Hershey Suite has a private entrance onto the inn's intimate garden courtyard, which is shaded by a century-old magnolia tree. Up the broad and winding central staircase, past a gal-

lery of family portraits, are located the remaining guest rooms—all of which are named after Civil War generals.

The highlight of a stay at Beechmont is breakfast, which is masterfully rendered by chef Susan. House specialties include an apricot puff pancake, a country egg dish concocted from potatoes, ham, sour cream, and cheese, a chocolate chip coffee cake, and a Beechmont baked apple topped with almonds.

BEECHMONT INN, 315 Broadway, Hanover, PA 17331; (717) 632-3013, (800) 553-7009; William and Susan Day, owners. Open all year. Seven rooms, all with private baths. Rates: $80 to $135 double with full breakfast. Children over 12 welcome; no pets, all major credit cards; no smoking. Fishing, riding, swimming, boating in state park; 3 public golf courses and many good antique shops in area. Many German country restaurants nearby.

DIRECTIONS: on Rte. 194 on north side of Hanover.

THE BRAFFERTON INN

Restoration in historic Gettysburg

In 1786, James Getty drew up plans for a new village to rise from the fertile farmlands of southern Pennsylvania. On the first deeded plot was built a sturdy and handsome fieldstone house, designed with deep-set windows, large and rambling rooms, and walls up to two-feet thick. As the oldest and most unusual dwelling in all of Gettysburg, the Brafferton Inn witnessed the life and times of this classic American village. The inn (then a private home) was called into duty during the Civil War, serving the community as a church when the local house of worship was pressed into service as a hospital. As battle raged outside the doors of the inn, a bullet found its way into a second-floor mantelpiece, and the wound remains there today.

Two years were spent restoring the house, adhering strictly to an eighteenth-century aesthetic, even commissioning well-known folk artist Virginia McLaughlin to paint a striking mural on the four walls of the dining room, depicting the buildings that made up early Gettysburg.

During renovation the attached house was purchased and a light-filled atrium was added to connect the two houses, at which point a fine bed and breakfast was born.

A hearty hot breakfast is served up each morning with specialties like mouth-watering apple-cinnamon pancakes and peaches-and-cream French toast being guest favorites.

Delightful and authentic in every aspect, the Brafferton Inn is an integral part of historic Gettysburg.

THE BRAFFERTON INN, 44–46 York Street, Gettysburg, PA 17325; (717) 337-3423; Sam and Jane Back, owners. Open all year. Ten rooms, all with private baths. Rates: $90 to $125 double, with full breakfast; $10 extra per child. Children over 9 welcome; no pets; Visa/MasterCard; smoking restricted to garden. Inn is in center of Gettysburg, within walking distance to restaurants.

DIRECTIONS: right off main traffic circle in downtown.

Early Gettysburg is depicted in a mural in the dining room.

A rustic guest room.

MARYLAND

INN AT ANTIETAM

On the edge of history

On September 17, 1862, 156,000 Union and Confederate soldiers waged the most intense one-day battle ever fought by Americans in any war. The Inn at Antietam sits right on the rim of this great battlefield, but today the fusillades of cannon fire have been replaced by the sounds of birds and soft winds blowing over lush farmland.

When Cal Fairbourn retired after a long and successful career as Vice President of Operations for the General Motors Acceptance Corporation, his wife Betty decided to start a career of her own. She wanted to fulfill a longtime dream of running a bed and breakfast inn. "Betty has given me moral support all our married life," said Cal. "I felt it was important for me to help her realize her goals." They bought and restored a 1908 home. Over the years they have lovingly added antique treasures, including an Amish buggy parked in the backyard, and turn-of-the-century beds, couches, and desks discovered at auctions and estate sales throughout the area.

Today the Fairbourns host many Civil War buffs who spend hours on the Antietam National Battlefield. But many others come for the peace and quiet of a country weekend, warmed by the smiles of a host and hostess who clearly love their new calling.

INN AT ANTIETAM. 220 East Main St., P.O. Box 119, Sharpsburg, MD 21782; (301) 432-6601; Cal and Betty N. Fairbourn, owners. Open February 14 through December 15. Four suites, three with queen beds and one with double, all with full private baths. Rates: $95 per room weekdays, $105 weekends (two-day minimum stays on weekends); includes full breakfast. Children over 6 welcome; no pets; no smoking; American Express.

DIRECTIONS: on Rte 34 on the edge of Sharpsburg.

Overleaf, the Lincoln portrait in the dining room commemorating the president's visit to the battlefield.

Left below, the dining room seen from the parlor.

A flowery guest room.

SPRING BANK INN

The rebirth of a stylish rural home

In 1880 gentleman farmer George Houck spared no expense when he built the most stylish home rural Frederick County had ever seen. Constructed of red brick, the house was given a Gothic Revival bay window, columned veranda, and gabled, fish-scale patterned slate roof. It was further embellished with elegant Italianate windows and an ornate belvedere for viewing the beautiful vistas of the surrounding countryside.

A century later the house captured the imaginations of Beverly and Ray Compton, who noticed it while on a bicycle tour of the area. Captivated as well by the rich history and architectural charms of Frederick, they soon bought Spring Bank Farm and embarked on a massive and much-needed restoration. Since the Comptons open bedrooms to overnight guests as each room is completed, today's guests are attending the birth of an inn and the rebirth of a house, with such fine details as frescoed ceilings, original brass hardware, louvered shutters, hand-marbled slate fireplaces, and hand-grained woodwork revealing themselves in the process.

Ray's family has been in the antiques business for several decades, and this expertise shows in many of Spring Bank's furnishings. High-ceilinged bedrooms easily accommodate full Victorian bedroom sets, canopied beds, and easy chairs. Plans are in the works to convert the third floor, which gives access to the belvedere, into an antiques shop.

SPRING BANK INN, 7945 Worman's Mill Rd., Frederick, MD 21701; (301) 694-0440, (800) 400-4667; Beverly and Ray Compton, hosts. Elegant 1880 rural home that combines Greek Revival and Italiante architecture. Open year-round. Five guest rooms, one with private bath. Rates $60–75 single, $70–95 double. Hearty continental breakfast. No children under twelve; no pets; no smoking in home; Visa/MasterCard/Discovery/American Express/checks. Appalachian trail close by; trout fishing; historic district to explore. Wide range of good restaurants in town.

DIRECTIONS: from I-70, I-270, or 340, take U.S. 15 north about 5 miles, driving past Frederick. Look for "mile 16" marker; turn right at next road onto Rte. 355 south. Inn is ¼ mile south on left.

NATIONAL PIKE INN

The antiques capital

"We're here and available," says Terry Rimel. "We give our guests as much hospitality as they want." At the National Pike Inn you can play the parlor organ, have breakfast in bed, and feel like a part of the family.

Conveniently located between Baltimore and Frederick, New Market has been dubbed the "Antiques Capital of Maryland." More than thirty antiques stores lure the collector here to shops specializing in folk art, clocks, early lighting, porcelain, jewelry, and Victorian furniture.

The guest rooms in the inn are air conditioned and provide fresh flowers and fruit. The Victorian Room has a four poster covered with a rosebud and mint-green chintz spread, a green tapestry Victorian settee, a Cheval mirror, and carved cherry wood dresser. The Canopy Room has steps leading up to its canopied bed, a chenille spread, a piecrust table, and fireside bench.

NATIONAL PIKE INN. 9–11 Main Street, P.O. Box 299, New Market, MD 21774; (301) 865-5055; Tom and Terry Rimel, hosts. Open all year. Four guest rooms and one suite, all with private baths. Rates: $75 to $160 includes full breakfast. Special weekly rates and on stays over two nights. Children over ten preferred; no pets; no smoking; Visa/MasterCard.

DIRECTIONS: from I-70 take exit 62 to Rte. 75 and go north 1 block to Main St. Take left on Main St. (Rte. 144) for about 3 blocks to top of hill to inn in center of town.

Right, innkeeper Norma Grovermann in front of the lovely Georgian building she and her husband have made into a delightful bed and breakfast.

PRINCE GEORGE INN

The first Annapolis bed and breakfast

Capital of the state of Maryland, and once capital of the nation, Annapolis is a mecca for history buffs, preservationists, seafood lovers, and sailors. The United States Naval Academy, St. John's College, art galleries, historic mansions, and Chesapeake Bay are all within walking distance of the Prince George Inn.

Historically correct in its loving restoration, the inn has been pampered by Bill and Norma Grovermann, two preservationists who fought to establish the first of Annapolis's bed and breakfasts. Charmingly decked out in Victoriana and all manner of ephemera, there are eye-catching details that intrigue, such as the large carved mirror which hung in the White House during the McKinley administration when Norma's grandfather was a jeweler to the White House. The "so Victorian" parlor boasts persimmon sofas, tufted velvet side chairs, nautical paintings, vintage photos, lacework, and peacock feathers garnered from birds raised by Norma's daughter.

Each of the four guest rooms is uniquely memorable, and one, a Turkish room, has a sultry feeling highlighted by twin brass beds, tapestries, ferns, hanging fans, an armoire, and intricate panels rescued from a mosque.

A deluxe continental breakfast buffet is served in the sunny, glassed-in side porch, and includes tasty treats that Norma creates. After breakfast, it is worth exploring the tiny corner "antique shop" near the breakfast room, that catches the spill-over of the Grovermann's "things you'd like to take home."

A spacious private garden, with a gazebo, adds another dimension to this 1884 Victorian Italianate house. It is no surprise that it is letter perfect. After all, it is one of a dozen houses that the Grovermanns have rescued and restored.

PRINCE GEORGE INN. 232 Prince George Street, Annapolis, MD 21401 (410) 263-6418; Bill and Norma Grovermann, owners. Open all year. Four guest rooms, 2 with private baths and 2 sharing. Rates: $75 to $95 per room, including full breakfast. Children 12 or over welcome; no pets; smoking restricted; Visa/MasterCard. Situated in Annapolis Historic District with 20 restaurants within walking distance. Naval Academy 2 blocks.

DIRECTIONS: inn is 3 blocks from harbor in downtown Annapolis.

An Oriental courtier and objets d'art.

A Thomas Sully painting of the wife of Dr. Skuhl of Philadelphia, with her first son and pregnant with her second child. She died in childbirth.

MR. MOLE

A treasure trove of objets d'art

"Mr. Mole" was an animal character in the beloved English children's book *The Wind in the Willows*, and the name suggests a warm, comfortable home. ·

And that is exactly what innkeepers Collin Clarke and Paul Bragaw have created in the historic Bolton Hill neighborhood. They have restored a spacious red-brick row house from the walls out and decorated the parlors and guest rooms with eighteenth and nineteenth-century antiques and a number of objets d'art surprises such as Oriental art, a statue of St. Peter, and nineteenth-century portraits.

There really is a Mr. Mole's House on the ground floor, with a separate street entrance. Its woodland décor recalls *The Wind in the Willows*. The London Suite offers a sitting room decorated in bold, bright

Left, the elegant parlor, painted in Kodak yellow.

colors of red and green, with Victorian graphics on the walls. The Explorer Suite displays eclectic treasures gathered from around the world. The other suites display similar imagination.

Many business people stay here because Mr. Mole is only a few minutes from the downtown area. Pleasure travelers enjoy being so close to Baltimore's Inner Harbor and Baltimore Orioles home games at Camden Yards.

Collin serves a "larger than continental breakfast," often with homemade cakes, pies, and breads. He believes in making city life as convenient as possible for guests and provides them with garage parking and an automatic garage door opener.

Mr. Mole has a whimsical name but a beautiful home.

MR. MOLE, 1601 Bolton Street, Baltimore, MD 21217; (410) 728-1179; Collin Clarke and Paul Bragaw, owners. French, German, Dutch spoken. Five suites, all with queen beds and private baths. Rates: $82 to $100 single, $97 to $140 double, includes continental-plus breakfast. Well-behaved children over 12 welcome; no pets; no smoking; all major credit cards.

DIRECTIONS: Call for directions.

The richness and warmth of the parlor.

HOPKINS INN

Four periods to choose from

The first room you notice is the charming parlor with its floral couch and matching wallpaper border, faux-finish mantel, etched-glass Victorian chandelier, handsome artworks, and lace panel curtains. Guests often relax here with a cup of coffee or a glass of wine.

The twenty-six guest rooms in this Spanish revival building have been arranged into four different periods: Federal, Victorian, Art Deco, and Contemporary. Guests are invited to reserve that period room that suits their mood or sense of fantasy.

Gray, lavender, peach, and blue offset the patterned rugs in the Federal room. The wallpaper border is a classical Adams frieze, and the mahogany armoire, Chippendale-style chairs, draped valances, and old prints enhance the period effect.

The Victorian room features a dressing mirror, wicker desk, white iron sweetheart bedstead, marble-topped tables, and lace curtains, while the Art Deco room has black lacquer furniture, Chinese-style lamps, twenties prints, and touches of period maroons and greys.

Finally, the contemporary room in browns and persimmon, accented in green, has a bed with brass headboard, rattan night stands, a pine armoire, and Hitchcock-style chair.

The monotony of the usual assemblage of small hotel rooms will not be found here; appointments do not smack of the decorator's art. Instead the charm of European bed and breakfasts and the warm hospitality of American country inns combines in a uniquely exciting blend.

HOPKINS INN. 3404 St. Paul Street, Baltimore, MD 21218; (410) 235-8600; Ona Speck, innkeeper. A historic building in a historic neighborhood. Open all year. Twenty-six guest rooms, including suites, all with private baths; some with kitchenettes. Rates: $85–$125. Continental breakfast. Children welcome; inquire about small pets; no smoking; major credit cards accepted. Within walking distance of Baltimore Museum of Art, one block from Johns Hopkins University.

DIRECTIONS: call for directions.

Truly a mansion.

GREEN SPRING VALLEY

A Cassatt family estate

Steeped in history, this secluded 26-room majestic estate, situated on 45 acres of Maryland's splendid Green Spring Valley, is just twenty minutes from Baltimore's Inner Harbor. Bed and breakfast is savored amidst the elegance enjoyed at the turn of the century.

It was built as a wedding gift for his daughter by Alexander J. Cassatt, president of the Pennsylvania Railroad and brother of Mary Cassatt, the impressionist painter. Later it became the home to descendants of Benjamin Franklin, and still later, the site of the Koinonia Foundation, a precursor of the Peace Corps, that trained people in literacy methods and organic gardening for service on every continent.

The house became a bed and breakfast shortly after it was purchased in 1985, and was furnished with choice antiques, beautiful artworks, and authentic period furniture. The baronial first floor has recessed paneling, beamed ceilings, huge fireplaces, a grand piano, oriental carpets, and that all-too-fast disappearing treasure, a library.

There are four elegant guest rooms: Aphrodite's Retreat, in shades of pink and mauve, sun-dappled and bedecked with French antiques; Aunt Mary's Suite, splendid in Victorian trappings with a canopied bed, fireplace, and claw-footed tub; the Ambassador's Room, a romantic guest room with intricate blue and gold wallpaper, fireplace, Jacuzzi, and elegant statuary shower; the Blue Garden Suite, a beautiful three-room suite with Louis XIV furniture, fireplace, and sun porch overlooking the olympic-sized pool.

Guests are welcome to swim in the pool, enjoy the hot tub, play tennis, visit the orchard, and the shitake mushroom plantings and herb gardens.

A gourmet breakfast served on fine china on the porch or by the fireplace in the dining room, depending on the season, features blackberries year round, a mushroom, tomato, and onion herb omelet, berry pancakes, and a vegetable dish delicacy.

In addition to all of the aforementioned bounty, this wonderful place and its engaging hosts are child friendly.

GREEN SPRING VALLEY. Five guest rooms with private baths. Open all year. Rates: $90 to $175 double, including full breakfast. Children welcome; no pets; no smoking. Good dining in area. *Represented by Amanda's Regional Reservation Service for Bed & Breakfast*, 1428 Park Avenue, Baltimore, MD 21217; (800) 899-7533; Fax (410) 728-8957; Betsy Grater. Visa/MasterCard/American Express/Discover.

DIRECTIONS: given on reservation.

The elegant dining room, set for breakfast.

TWIN GATES B&B

Bach with breakfast

Twin Gates is only fifteen minutes north of Baltimore's exciting Inner Harbor, but it seems a world removed. The surrounding grounds are lush, expansive, and private. Gwen and Bob Vaughan decorated the house using a palette of soft blue, peach, cream, and beige. The first-floor common rooms, with fourteen-foot ceilings, feel spacious, and the inn's old-fashioned front porch, furnished with white wicker and bedecked with the flags of the U.S. and Maryland, provide an added dimension of charm and comfort. Each bedroom is furnished with every thoughtful amenity, from extra pillows and blankets to a homebaked "sweet dream" on pillows at night.

Gwen shines in the kitchen each morning, concocting such delectibles as strawberry shortcake or peach-and-orange-drenched French toast, known as "fuzzy navel." Early evening finds Bob in charge of the wine and cheese hour, during which guests recuperate from the rigors of the day and enjoy relaxed conversation.

TWIN GATES BED & BREAKFAST INN. 308 Morris Avenue, Lutherville, MD 21093; (410) 252-3131. Bob and Gwen Vaughn, hosts. Open all year. Six guest rooms, all with private baths and queen beds. Rates: $95 to $145 per room, include a full "heart-smart" breakfast. Children over 12 welcome; no pets; smoking permitted only on the porches or in the gardens; all major credit cards.

DIRECTIONS: use Exit 25 north (Charles St.) from the Baltimore Beltway (I-695). Take immediate right on Bellona Avenue for 3 blocks to Morris Avenue.

WHITE SWAN TAVERN

Stay the night in a comfortable museum

A stay at the White Swan is rewarding because guests can feel the care the inn has been given. The main floor contains three parlors, or sitting rooms. The formal and dignified Joseph Nicholson Room, named after the second owner of the property, is furnished from Mr. Nicholson's inventory, a document unearthed during research. The Isaac Cannell Room is filled with game tables appropriate to the days when it was an integral part of the original tavern.

Bedrooms are decorated in several styles. Three are done in formal colonial: one with pencil post twin beds, one with a lace canopied double bed, and one with cannonball four-posters. All have wing chairs for reading, fresh colors, and beautiful hardwood floors. The T.W. Elliason Suite has been restored to its Victorian origins. The bedroom and separate sitting room are decorated with high-back massive beds, a tufted settee, decorative friezes, and a busy floral carpet.

The White Swan's continental breakfast is special because it employs the talents of a gifted local baker and includes fresh-squeezed orange juice and grapefruit juice. Served in the Isaac Cannell Room, guests may request that breakfast be delivered to their door instead.

Chestertown, an important seaport in the early 1700s, is one of those special American towns that still reflects its moment of prosperity. The seat of Kent County and the home of Washington College, the town retains a great measure of grace and atmosphere.

WHITE SWAN TAVERN, 231 High St., Chestertown, MD 21620; (410) 778-2300, Fax (410) 778-4543; Mary Susan Maisel, hostess. Open all year. Six guest rooms in house, one attached "summer kitchen" suite, all private baths. Rates: $100 to $150, double occupancy; $25 per extra occupant; rates include light breakfast. Good dining nearby, especially in season. Children welcome; no pets; no credit cards. Area offers local museums, walking tours, recreation, wildlife preserves.

DIRECTIONS: from Chesapeake Bay Bridge (Rte. 50-301), take Rte. 301N to Rte. 213. Turn left on Rte. 213. Turn left on Rte. 213 to Chestertown, approx. 15 miles. Cross the Chester River Bridge and turn left at first stop light (Cross St.). Turn left again at next light (High St.). Inn is in middle of block on right.

Lovegrove's kitchen is the oldest and most rustic of the guest rooms.

1886 carved detail gives the building's date.

VANDIVER INN

The mayor's house

A beautiful three-story Queen Anne home was built in 1886 for Murray Vandiver, then mayor of Havre de Grace, Maryland. This regal mansion with five chimneys, eight fireplaces, and large high-ceilinged rooms must have projected the appropriate sense of power and grace because Mr. Vandiver rose rapidly in the political world.

Today you can enjoy many of the same Victorian pleasures as the Mayor and his privileged guests did then in the mansion, which is now on the National Historic Register. Stay in one of five antiques-furnished guest rooms, two with working fireplaces. Each room is named after a famous Marylander. The Millard Tydings Room with its 1890 bed with a high mahogany backboard is a favorite of honeymooners. Other travelers choose the John Rodgers Room with its huge ornate tiled fireplace and other period antiques, including a melodeon—a small reed organ popular in the U.S. in the 1850s. The staff ensures that the "mayor's guests" enjoy every moment of their stay, including candlelit breakfasts by the fireplace in the spacious dining room. Dinner is served on weekends and guests order such house specialties as filet mignon topped with bleu cheese herb crust and sweet-n-spicy shrimp.

An art nouveau objets d'art cabinet in the Walbert Room.

VANDIVER INN, 301 S. Union Ave., Havre de Grace, MD 21078; (410) 939-5200; Robert and Sarah Scardina, innkeepers. Open all year. Eight rooms, all with double beds and private baths. Rates: $75 to $125 per room, with corporate rates available Sunday to Thursday. Full gourmet breakfast included. Children over 12 welcome; no pets; Visa/MasterCard/American Express; smoking is limited. Located five blocks from the Chesapeake Bay and the 1827 Concord Point Lighthouse, the oldest continuously operating lighthouse on the East Coast. The Decoy Museum and a row of antique stores are nearby.

DIRECTIONS: take I-95 to Rte. 155 east into Havre de Grace onto Otsego Street. Follow to its end at Union Avenue and turn right and go seven blocks to the Inn on the left.

Left above, the Millard Tydings Room, with its 1890 bed. Below, the period sitting room.

The inn's museum displays wedding shoes.

THE PARSONAGE INN B&B

In the exquisite town of St. Michaels

Imposingly set on the main street.

St. Michael's, Maryland, is known locally as the town that "fooled the British." During the War of 1812, townspeople strung lanterns on trees away from St. Michaels when a British fleet approached. That night the fleet mistook the lights for the town and bombarded some trees into pulp, saving St. Michaels. Tourists today are not so easily distracted. Many head for the superb Chesapeake Bay Maritime Museum, the antiques shops, and restaurants that serve wonderful Maryland crab every which way—in cakes, steamed, and in soups and salads.

The Parsonage Inn was built in 1883 as a private residence for a local businessman. It was donated to the United Methodist Church in the 1920's and served as the church's parsonage house until 1985 when it was purchased by Willard Workman and his son.

A breakfast of Belgian waffles.

As they began to remodel this home, they realized they were working with an almost perfect example of Victorian architecture—paneled chimneys, porches lined with gingerbread woodwork, and high ceilinged rooms with working fireplaces. To be true to the period, they added Queen Anne-style furnishings while at the same time bowing to modern tastes by adding to each of the eight guest rooms private baths, central heat and air conditioning, and queen or king-sized brass beds adorned with Laura Ashley linens.

Today guests gather in the parlor to check menus of some of the famous restaurants nearby, such as the Ashley Room at the Inn At Perry Cabin (owned by Lord Ashley and the Laura Ashley Company), and The Talbot.

A guest room.

After breakfast of various gourmet dishes plus a selection of homemade pastries and jams served with tea or freshly-ground coffee in the candlelit dining room, guests can borrow 12-speed bicycles to peddle down the nearby flat roads along the coast. Others enjoy taking a cruise (April through October) for a tour of magnificent, columned mansions along the Miles River, an arm of Chesapeake Bay.

THE PARSONAGE INN BED & BREAKFAST, 210 N. Talbot St., St. Michaels, MD 21663; (800) 394-5519; Willard Workman, owner. Open all year. Eight guest rooms with private baths and a parlor and dining room open to guests. Rates: $70 to $120 single, $80 to $130 double, with gourmet breakfast included. Accepts children of all ages; no pets; smoking not permitted; Visa/MasterCard.

DIRECTIONS: take Rte. 50 to Easton/Rte. 322 bypass. Take Rte. 33 west approximately nine miles to main street of St. Michaels (Talbot St.) Parking in the rear of the inn or on the street.

The view on Talbot Street.

Innkeeper Thelma Driscoll in one of the restored, luxuriously appointed guest rooms.

CHANCEFORD HALL

A dream come true

Chanceford Hall is virtually a dream come true, since it embodies all of the attributes we list on the back cover of this book as reasons people like to go to bed and breakfasts—interesting architecture, fascinating history, friendly hosts, scenic surroundings, reasonable rates, and sumptuous breakfasts.

The affable but determined hosts spared nothing in personally restoring the neglected mansion to perfection. Michael even sewed the drapes and made the antique reproduction furniture in his workshop on the premises, while Thelma laboriously freed the exquisite, handcarved detailing throughout the house from accumulated layers of paint.

The large dining room, with its beautiful furnishings, sets the scene for exceptional breakfasts, but the hosts will also serve dinners there to inn guests by prior arrangement. Beside a crackling fire on cool evenings, five-course dinners are served with sterling silver, Waterford crystal, and antique Limoges china. Given enough notice, any menu is possible, with the ingredients even being flown in on occasion.

CHANCEFORD HALL, 209 West Federal Street, Snow Hill, MD 21863; (301) 632-2231; Michael and Thelma Driscoll, owners. Open all year. Five guest rooms with private baths, 4 with working fireplaces. Rates: $110 to $130, including full breakfast. Well behaved children over 12; no pets; no credit cards (personal checks accepted). Swimming pool on premises; country club golfing nearby. Recommended dining at Evelyn's Village Inn Country Restaurant and The Upper Deck in Pocomoke City.

DIRECTIONS: from Annapolis take U.S. 50 down the Chesapeake Peninsula to Salisbury and follow Rte. 12 all the way to Federal Street through Snow Hill. Watch for sign on lawn of inn

VIRGINIA

The piano is a much-used part of the living room.

LIBERTY ROSE

A Williamsburg jewel

When Colonial Williamsburg was being restored in the late 1920s, a two-story frame and brick house flanked by beech, oak, and poplar trees had already been built a few years earlier atop a nearby hill about a mile from the historic area.

In 1986 Brad and Sandi Hirz arrived in Williamsburg with their own dreams for a really posh bed and breakfast. Sandi had been an interior decorator in California and taught doll-making as an avocation. Brad had been a farmer in Washington State. Combining their aptitudes for art and hard work, they turned the dormered, twin-chimnied colonial home into a bed and breakfast masterpiece.

Each of the four guest rooms seems like an antique valentine for lovers of all ages. A canopied carved

Built in the 1920s.

Left, the Rose Victoria Room has a French antique canopied bed.

ball and claw poster bed, swathed in silk and Jacquard fabrics, is the elegant star of the Williamsburg Suite. Not to be out-done, the Rose Victoria guest room has an antique tin ceiling and a cherry French canopied bed with pull-down colonial drapes handmade by Sandi with some advice from a Williamsburg seamstress. The Magnolia Peach also has a canopied bed and a cherry armoire. Savannah Lace lives up to its luxurious name with lace-draped windows.

Add to these romantic settings English and French antiques throughout the house, cushy bathrobes for the guests, private baths with bubble bath fixings and you know just a few of the reasons why Liberty Rose has won numerous awards.

Sandi still loves dolls. There is at least one on every bed welcoming ladies with a single rose.

LIBERTY ROSE. 1022 Jamestown Road, Williamsburg, VA 23185; (800) 545-1825 or (804) 253-1260; Sandi and Brad Hirz, innkeepers. Four rooms, all with private baths and Queen-sized beds, one with small adjoining room with twin bed for a third person; claw foot tubs or marble showers; two rooms have both. Rates: $110 to $185, including full gourmet breakfast. Children over 12 welcome; no pets; no smoking; Visa/MasterCard/American Express. Excellent variety of restaurants within a short drive, from colonial cuisine to Thai, Chinese, and continental. Walk or drive to nearby Colonial Williamsburg.

DIRECTIONS: from I-64, take exit 242A for 5 miles to Jamestown Road (also called Rte. 5) and go right about ½ mile. Home is on your left. From Colonial Williamsburg (where Jamestown Road meets Merchants Square), take Jamestown Road 1 ⅓ mile. Liberty Rose is on your right.

The bathroom to the Rose Victoria Room.

Right, Sandi and Brad Hirz.

The Savannah Lace Room's bathroom.

MUNCY & MUNCY PHOTOGRAPH

Edgewood's guest rooms are a joy for antiques collectors.

EDGEWOOD PLANTATION

Romantically swathed in linens and laces

"Old Virginia" is embodied in Edgewood Plantation, one of the surviving manor homes that front on the James River. Built in 1849 by northerner Spencer Rowland, it is in the Carpenter Gothic style that only became popular in the South thirty years later.

The aura of the Civil War still clings to the house. Its tower was used as a lookout, and General Jeb Stuart of the Confederate Army stopped here on his way to Richmond to warn General Robert E. Lee about the Union's strength. Still etched in her bedroom window is the name of Rowland's daughter, Lizzie, who is said to have died of a broken heart while waiting for her lover to return from the war.

The plantation has fourteen large and beautiful guest rooms, romantically swathed in heirloom linens and laces that provide every finery and elegance to satisfy the most avid seeker of ante-bellum living. There is a honeymoon suite, a Victorian Room, a Civil War Room, and of course Scarlett's Room, among others. Each is the best room to stay in.

A full country breakfast in the formal dining room is enhanced by candlelight and is elegantly served by truly gracious southern hosts Dot and Julian Boulware. During the holidays the house is aglow with eighteen trimmed Christmas trees—a spectacular sight.

EDGEWOOD PLANTATION, 4800 John Taylor Hwy, Charles City, VA 23030; (800) 296-3343, (804) 829-2962; Julian and Dot Boulware, owners. Open all year. 8 guest rooms, all with private baths. Rates: $120 to $188 per room, including full Southern breakfast. No children; no pets; smoking restricted; Visa/Mastercard. Swimming pool, tavern, antiques shop, gift shop, 1725 grist mill, English gardens. Wonderful dining at 5-star restaurants in area. Between Williamsburg and Richmond, there are famous plantations to visit, with special tours at Christmas.

DIRECTIONS: from Washington take I-95 to Richmond and take Rte. 295, following James River plantation to Rte. 5. Take Charles City exit and go 12 miles to inn on left.

Breakfast in the Gazebo.

An English garden surrounds the Gazebo.

MISS MOLLY'S INN

On fabulous Chincoteague Island

Separated from the bustling Virginia mainland by the Chesapeake Bay, Miss Molly's Inn on Chincoteague Island captures the hearts of all who stay here. Built by J. T. Rowley, the local oyster king, the house was inhabited by his daughter "Miss Molly" when Chincoteague and neighboring Assateague Island were linked to the Eastern shore.

The Chincoteague National Wildlife Refuge and the chestnut and mocha wild beach ponies that roam here freely became a drawing card for tourists. Once a year, on the last Thursday of July, the ponies are rounded up in a holding pen and driven out into the bay to swim to Chincoteague Island. There they are herded down Main Street to the carnival grounds where unabashed horse lovers gather to admire them. Marguerite Henry's popular book *Misty of Chincoteague Island* was written in the 1940s while she was vacationing at Miss Molly's.

This grand thirteen-room house was lovingly restored and furnished with a generous dose of Victoriana: overstuffed chairs, lace curtains, claw-footed tubs, and old wicker.

Blueberry pancakes and sausage, or bagels and smoked salmon, are typical morning fare. English afternoon tea, served on the veranda or in the gazebo, features host Barbara Wiedenhefts' worlds-best scones.

Fluent in French, Dutch, and German, the Yorkshire-born hostess came to America to work at the British Embassy. After meeting her Chicago-born husband, David, at a dinner party, they embarked on a new adventure—running a romantic bed and breakfast inn.

Guests have had their loyalty tested on more than one occasion. During Hurricane Gloria, four honeymoon couples happened to be staying at the inn. All of them pitched in to carry every bit of furniture, including heavy Victorian settees, to the second floor. Fortunately, flooding didn't occur.

MISS MOLLY'S INN, Chincoteague, VA 23336; (804) 336-6686; Barbara and David Wiedenheft, owners. Open March through New Year's. Seven great guest rooms, 5 with private baths and 2 sharing. Rates: $69 to $145 per room, including full breakfast and English afternoon tea. Children over 8 welcome; no pets; no smoking; Visa/Mastercard. There are 27 restaurants nearby, including one 4-star. Island activities: crabbing, sailing, surfing, swimming on natural beach.

DIRECTIONS: from Norfolk take US-13 north to Rte. 175 to causeway to Main Street on Chincoteague Island. Inn is 2½ blocks north of Main Street. From Washington take US-50 south to US-13 and proceed to Rte. 175.

Left, Smithfield's waterfront. Above, more treasures at the outdoor markets.

ISLE OF WIGHT INN

A fine place to stay

Smithfield, famous for succulent hams, is situated in a very historic part of Virginia near Chesapeake Bay, not far from Williamsburg. One national shrine that is an integral part of Smithfield's history is St. Luke's Church, founded in 1632, the oldest English-speaking church in America.

There are also wonderful, historic houses to visit in Smithfield, two of which belong to the owners of the inn. Sam Earl's house is a 1780 brick Colonial that can be seen on the organized house tours. Bob Hart's 1900 white-columned, seventeen-room Queen Anne mansion is one of the most imposing sights in town, especially when his 1939 black Packard is parked in the driveway.

Sam is a retired NASA engineer whose specialty is clockmaking and antiques, which explains the quality of the inn's fine antiques shop.

The inn itself is a relatively new building, but the décor of the dining room is traditional. There, continental breakfast is served, with one tasty improvement—Smithfield ham.

The guest rooms are located in a two-story wing which is comfortable and functional, with all rooms individually decorated. Some have four-poster beds and several larger suites have fireplaces. One special suite has a Jacuzzi.

Altogether, Smithfield has a relaxed, leisurely atmosphere, with open-air art exhibits and waterfront marinas and docks adding to the festive mood.

ISLE OF WIGHT INN, 1607 South Church Street, Smithfield, VA 23430; (804) 357-3176; Sam Earl and Bob Hart, owners. Open all year. Eight guest rooms with private baths, air conditioning, and cable TV. Rates: $52 to $79 single, $59 to $79 double, including full breakfast. Children welcome; no pets; smoking allowed in some rooms; Visa/Mastercard/American Express/Discover. Several nice restaurants nearby.

DIRECTIONS: one mile east of downtown Smithfield on Rte. 10, near south end of James River bridge.

Treasures in the inn's antiques shop.

The living Room is beautifully restored.

THE HUTZLER HOUSE

On Richmond's Monument Avenue

Many say that Richmond's Monument Avenue, guarded by huge statues of Confederate heroes, is one of the prettiest in the South. The Emanuel Hutzler House was a stately addition when built on the wide, tree-lined boulevard in 1914. In the past three years this 8,000 square foot bed and breakfast has been totally and painstakingly restored by its present owners, Lyn Benson and John Richardson.

Their goal was to return the building to its elegant Italian Renaissance style. The natural mahogany raised panels in the entry, the marble fireplace in the large living room, flanked by beautiful mahogany bookcases, and the restored original flooring all testify to how well Lyn and John have succeeded.

There are four guest rooms, each competing to be more unusual and attractive than the others. The front suite overlooks Monument Avenue and pampers guests with a Jacuzzi tub and a marble fireplace. All of the rooms have queen beds, private baths, and soothing pastel colors. Many guests are surprised at first by the vivid hunter-red on the walls of the Marion Room, but John says guests often leave saying, "I'm going to use this color at home." The pleasures of staying in the Emanuel Hutzler House are monumental.

THE EMANUEL HUTZLER HOUSE. 2036 Monument Avenue, Richmond, VA 23220; (804) 353-6900; Lyn Benson and John Richardson, hosts. Open all year. Four rooms with private baths and phones. Rates: $85 to $125 single, $89 to $139 double, with full gourmet breakfast. Children over 12 welcome; no pets; no smoking; Visa/ Mastercard/American Express. The hosts have a large collection of menus from local restaurants that they share with guests. Near many local activities and attractions, including Civil War battlefields, the White House and the Museum of the Confederacy.

DIRECTIONS: take exit 78 off I-64 to Boulevard and turn right for one mile to Broad. Go left on Broad for ½ mile and right on Meadow for 2 blocks to Monument and right again.

Left, Robert E. Lee dominates Richmond's Monument Avenue.

The 1914 townhouse.

The richly paneled entrance hall.

A natural paradise of lush flower gardens and fruitful vineyards.

HIGH MEADOWS INN

Vineyard country

In 1953, the tornado that hit High Meadows lifted its entire porch off and deposited it intact near the pond. Almost thirty years later, Peter Sushka and M. Jae Abbitt purchased this neglected property, restored it to Historic Landmark status, and planted a Pinot Noir and Chardonnay vineyard to boot. In 1989 guests helped them harvest their first grapes.

Sitting smartly on a twenty-two acre estate, the house is complemented by gardens of antique roses. Seven guest rooms, uniquely furnished with antiques, have lacy comforters, heart-shaped pillows, Oriental and American floor coverings, festoon curtains, original botanicals, and steel engravings. There is a Federal parlor, a Victorian music room, a grand hall, and an inviting west terrace.

Breakfast includes a variety of tasty egg dishes, homemade breads and muffins, fresh fruit, and coffee or tea. Wonderful European supper baskets are available, overflowing with everything from lasagna, quiche, salads, and mousse . . . to roses and books of poetry.

Just minutes south of Charlottesville, on Route 20, the inn is along the same road that Jefferson traveled to visit his brother. Monticello, Jefferson's home, as well as the presidential homes of Madison and Monroe are nearby. The historic town of Scottsville, the University of Virginia, and wine tasting tours are other popular attractions.

After visiting High Meadows for a long weekend and partaking of afternoon tea and early evening tastings of local wines, a recent guest's comment seems particularly apt:

"Our three-day stay was a delight from start to finish. Many thanks and we'll be back."

So will you.

HIGH MEADOWS INN, Rte 4, Box 6, Scottsville, VA 24590; (804) 286-2218; Peter Sushka and Mary Jae Abbitt, owners. Open all year. Twelve spacious rooms with private baths. Rates: $79 to $155 per room, including full country breakfast; Sat. $175 to $235, including wine tasting, hors d'oeuvres, and 6-course dinner. Children over 8 welcome; pets by special advance arrangement; no smoking; Visa/Mastercard. Tours of vineyards in heart of Virginia's wine country. Antiquing and James River activities.

DIRECTIONS: from Charlottesville take Rte. 20 south (exit 24 off I-64) and go past Monticello for 17.6 miles; watch for High Meadows sign and turn left.

LAMBSGATE

A country experience for urbanites

After years of bed and breakfasting in England and Scotland, Dan and Elizabeth Fannon decided to combine British know-how with native Virginia hospitality. On seven pastoral acres in the Shenandoah Valley and along with twenty woolly lambs, they offer urbanites the ultimate country experience. Sitting on the verandah of this 1816 farmhouse in an old wicker rocker, one can watch the sun set behind the Alleghanies or remark on the cows crossing the road. For the more actively inclined, the sheep like to be petted.

Dan, the upstairs maid and breakfast chef, delights in spreading a bountiful country breakfast in the family dining room. Country ham, bacon, eggs, grits, muffins, and toast are regulars. Sometimes he serves his specialty—ginger pancakes with strawberry sauce.

Three guest rooms have bucolic views: the room with the big oak armoire that faces the mountain; the room with red and white polka dots and

Left, woolly ewes before their April shearing.

The River Room.

sheepskin throw, that overlooks the pasture; and a room with stenciled wallpaper where the Middle River can be seen—when it rises high enough.

Everything is comfortable and cozy, and with the lambs ba-baaing it is a perfect antidote to burnout.

LAMBSGATE BED & BREAKFAST, Rte. 1 Box 63, Swoope, VA 24479; (703) 337-6929; Elizabeth and Daniel Fannon, owners. Open all year; 3 guest rooms (1 with twin beds) share 1 bath. Rates: $41.95 single, $52.55 double, including full country breakfast. Children welcome; no pets, no smoking; no credit cards, but personal checks accepted. Historic area, including Museum of American Frontier Culture, Woodrow Wilson's birthplace. Recommended restaurants nearby at McCormick's Pub & Restaurant and Rowe's Family Restaurant.

DIRECTIONS: near Staunton; call for brochure with map.

The Pastures Room.

The Holt Room.

Flying staircase built when the second story was added circa 1840.

THE SAMPSON EAGON INN

Picture perfect

Stepping into a guest room at the antebellum Sampson Eagon Inn is like walking into a period portrait. Each room is named after a different family member connected with the house and is decorated with antiques from different eras of American history—rice-carved four poster canopied beds, a nineteenth-century desk with secret compartments, Victorian fainting couches, and balloon curtains. A unique free-standing spiral staircase winds majestically from the entrance way to the second floor. Woodrow Wilson (born in a house almost directly across the street) would have felt right at home in the elegant formal living room and dining room. .

The inn has been "discovered" by a number of national magazines such as *Gourmet* and *Southern Living*, who extolled the setting and the décor. Innkeeper Laura Mattingly says, "We've tried to create a home that has a sense of historic elegance with

Left below, a breakfast of soufflé pancakes with Grand Marnier orange sauce and baked apple.

the feel of home." Her full breakfasts include such specialties as soufflé pancakes served with an orange/Grand Marnier sauce that is divine. Her husband, Frank, has personally done most of the restoration, starting with a bare shell of a house and ending with an inn that radiates the good life, Victorian style. Laura and Frank genuinely enjoy people, and the friendship begins the minute guests open the large front door.

THE SAMPSON EAGON INN, 238 E. Beverly St., Staunton, VA 24401; (800) 597-9722, (540) 886-8200; Laura and Frank Mattingly, innkeepers. Open all year. Two suites with queen-size canopied beds and separate sitting rooms with a twin-size day bed. Three guest rooms with canopied queen-size beds. All rooms have TV/VCR's and private modern baths. Rates: $80 to $95 single (available Sun. to Thurs. only), $85 to $99 double, $15 for extra person in suite; includes full gourmet breakfast. Suitable for children 12 years and older; no pets; smoking restricted to porch and garden; personal and travelers checks or cash but no credit cards. The Woodrow Wilson Birthplace and Presidential Museum is right across the street (don't miss his 1919 Pierce-Arrow presidential limousine on display). Walk to the downtown area and numerous restaurants.

DIRECTIONS: take exit 222 or 225 off I-81 and follow brown signs to the Woodrow Wilson birthplace that will lead you right to the inn.

The antique square piano in the parlor.

HIDDEN VALLEY B&B

Show time in the country

A guest room.

Imagine an antebellum mansion with Hollywood movie star Richard Gere galloping by on horseback every evening while Jodie Foster sits prettily near a fireside burning merrily under a huge wooden mantel.

That's the kind of excitement bed and breakfast hosts Ron and Pam Stidham experienced firsthand for several months as the movie *Sommersby* was filmed in their home and in the surrounding George Washington National Forest. The U.S. Forest Service had originally purchased this 1848 home and the surrounding 8,000 acres in 1985. Then Ron and Pam negotiated a landmark lease with the Forest Service, which gave them the right to operate a bed and breakfast establishment in their home.

The Stidhams started a complete restoration of the

Left, the inn seen from the trout stream.

The gorgeous elegantly formal inn, with the museum on the right.

Greek Revival home in 1990 and the Sommersby film crew added some finishing touches, including a row of authentic slave cabins transplanted from West Virginia. They even created a replica of a nineteenth-century summer kitchen, now part of a permanent museum next to the mansion.

Today guests can lounge on the front porch, walk forest trails, fish in the Jackson River (known world-wide as a mecca for trout fishermen) just a few yards in front of the house, and visit some of the historic and scenic attractions within an easy drive.

The house is truly a mansion in every sense of that word, with gorgeous trappings that include a marblelized fireplace, a formal dining room and three guest rooms, two with queen-size beds and one with two double beds. Each is furnished with eighteenth and nineteenth-century antiques.

HIDDEN VALLEY BED & BREAKFAST. Hidden Valley Rd., Warm Springs, VA 24484; (540) 839-3178; Ron and Pam Stidham, innkeepers. Three guest rooms, with private baths. Rates: $79 to $89 double, including full breakfast. Children over 6 welcome; inquire about separate area for pets; smoking on outside porches only; no credit cards.

DIRECTIONS: in George Washington National Forest. Look for Hidden Valley sign on US-220 north of Warm Springs.

The rebuilt kitchen fireplace in the museum.

Over two centuries of history.

Guests return year after year.

ANDERSON COTTAGE B&B

Near the famous Warm Springs spa

Even if they never had a grandmother who lived in the country, many people daydream about the pleasures of visiting the rural home she *might* have had. This would be a home where they could sit on a wide wraparound porch overlooking a flower bed, wade in a shallow creek fed by warm waters from hot underground springs, and relax with handsome farm furniture without fear of scratching a highly-polished antique.

That's the comfortable grandmotherly atmosphere maintained by innkeeper Jean Randolph Bruns at the log-and-clapboard Anderson Cottage, now over 200 years old. Every piece in the house seems to have its own story, from the antique piano in the dining room to the scarred old original fireplace mantels. Breakfast is served in the dining room, with a fire crackling in the fireplace on chilly days. The hostess, a former newspaper reporter and bureau chief, has collected thousands of books guests can enjoy in their rooms or on that wide porch.

Many of the guests are repeat visitors who come to hike in the woods, visit the historic Warm Springs spa that offers bathing in 96 degree waters, or attend the Garth Newel Music Center for a chamber music concert. They can also drive to three recreational lakes about thirty minutes away.

Many are repeat guests who return year after year to visit with Jean in her wonderful old home. And, yes, she really *is* a grandmother.

ANDERSON COTTAGE BED & BREAKFAST, Old Germantown Road, Box 176, Warm Springs, VA 24484-0176; (540) 839-2975; Jean Randolph Bruns, innkeeper. Two suites (bedrooms and parlors) and two guest rooms in the main house; two bedrooms in the next-door kitchen cottage with kitchen/dining living room area that is ideal for families. The main house is closed December through March; the kitchen cottage open year-round. Rates: $60 to $110 single or double, including full breakfast. Main house is not recommended for children but they are welcome in the kitchen cottage; bringing pets is negotiable; English and some French spoken; no credit cards—checks accepted.

DIRECTIONS: stay on Rte. 39 to Warm Springs; at foot of mountain go about ¼ mile to Old Germantown Road (Rte. 692).

The parlor, with the original fireplace.

An imposing mansion.

LYNCHBURG MANSION

Past luxuries brought to life

The inn brochure promises that this is a bed and breakfast "where you can return to the finer yesterday."

But it's hard to imagine the past could equal the luxury hosts Bob and Mauranna Sherman have created for their guests at the Lynchburg Mansion Inn. Granted, they began with a beautiful columned Spanish Georgian mansion built in 1914 for a local coal and bank magnate. But today each room is a showcase of interior design.

You enter through double doors into a massive Grand Hall with high ceilings and paneled cherry wainscoting. To your right is the parlor where guests can relax in a beautiful setting created by a fireplace, antique piano, and Victorian era antiques and reproductions.

The guest rooms continue the journey into a "finer past." The Gilliam Room has a king-size four-poster mahogany bed with steps. The Bown Room has a country French décor with a queen-size four-poster, a huge armoire, and an Aubusson rug. The Veranda Suite has a large bedroom with a king-size bed and

Left, innkeeper Bob Sherman preparing the formal breakfast room.

a kitchenette. This suite opens onto a circular veranda that seems appropriate for a latter-day Scarlett O'Hara and Rhett Butler.

Guests can soak in a bubbling hot-tub spa right outside the back door, read in an atrium sun room, and then explore the brick-paved streets of Lynchburg's historic district.

LYNCHBURG MANSION INN BED & BREAKFAST. 405 Madison St., Lynchburg, VA 24504, (800) 352-1199 or (804) 528-5400; Bob and Mauranna Sherman, innkeepers. Open all year. Three guest rooms and two suites with full private baths. Rates: $84 to $114 single, $89 to $119 double, including a full gourmet breakfast. Children are welcome; no pets; smoking on outside veranda only; Visa/MasterCard/American Express/Diners Club.

DIRECTIONS: 3 hours south of Washington, D.C. from Rte. 29 south, take Main Street exit and turn left on Fifth St. and turn right on Madison St.

A guest room.

THE MANOR AT TAYLOR'S STORE

Gourmet nutrition

The inn's name calls for an explanation. Taylor's Store, once a trading post for settlers heading west, is long gone. The Manor House, built on the site, and once the centerpiece of a large and prosperous tobacco plantation, has been restored to its former elegance by Lee and Mary Lynn Tucker.

Six well appointed suites are masterfully blended in period furnishings, and there is a charming garden cottage, ideal for families with children or couples vacationing together. Guest rooms include the Victorian Suite, romantic in rose; the Colonial Suite in Williamsburg blue with a private balcony to view memorable sunsets; the Plantation Suite with antebellum furnishings; and the English Garden Suite with its private entrance.

Breakfast at the Manor is as healthful as it is delicious. Mary Lynn is a nutritionist and both she and her pathologist husband are gourmet cooks who delight in serving up whole wheat pancakes, Canadian bacon, soufflés, quiche, or waffles. Guests eat off elegant china and silver plate in the formal dining room, but a few have been known to eat in the country kitchen while visiting the chef.

A hot tub in the basement, a glass-paneled solarium, an exercise room, a den, and a billiard room are prized amenities, and there is talk of turning the old grainery on the premises into an art gallery for local artists. There are 100 acres of recreational woodlands and ponds, swimming and fishing, and the Blue Ridge foothills that provide God's incomparable backdrop.

THE MANOR AT TAYLOR'S STORE, Rte 1, Box 533, Smith Mountain Lake, VA 24184; (800) 248-6267, (540) 721-3951; Fax (540) 721-5243; Lee and Mary Lynn Tucker, owners. Open all year; 9 guest rooms, 7 with private baths, 2 share; cottage with 3 bedrooms and 2 baths rents as a unit. Rates: $80 to $170 per room, including healthful gourmet breakfast. Children welcome in cottage; no pets; no smoking in house; a little German spoken. Fine dining in area, including 8 restaurants featuring seafood.

DIRECTIONS: from Roanoke or Blue Ridge Parkway take Rte. 220 south to Rocky Mount and Rte. 122 east to inn.

Mary Lynn and Lee Tucker with their restored manor house.

WASHINGTON, D.C.

KALORAMA GUEST HOUSE

A cosmopolitan clientele from around the world

Hidden away from the bustle of the city on a quiet residential street, the Kalorama Guest House is a home away from home. Its thirty-one well appointed rooms are put together with a cozy mix of fine antiques and grandmother's attic that includes beautiful Victorian bedsteads, armoires, and old Singer sewing machines that have been converted to tables.

PHOTOGRAPHS BY MICHAEL ACH

Wrought iron park benches serve as seating for breakfast in the brick-walled dining room.

Vintage photographs, old advertising prints, and portraits decorate the walls, and vases of fresh flowers lend fragrance and color to the public rooms. A generous continental breakfast is served in the brick-walled dining room where wrought iron park benches beside marble top tables afford guests from around the world the opportunity to meet and converse. Friendships can be furthered sipping afternoon sherry before a crackling fire.

Holidays are taken seriously here with a party at Halloween, stockings hung in guest rooms at Christmas, and baskets delivered to all at Easter. The fun-loving staff is attentive, friendly, and always ready to help with directions for sightseeing or museum going. Located in the Adams Morgan section, a vibrant neighborhood of old townhouses, antiques shops, and ethnic restaurants, the Kalorama is a five-minute taxi ride from downtown and all that Washington has to offer.

Noteworthy architectural details highlight a substantial old building.

THE KALORAMA GUEST HOUSE at Kalorama Park, 1854 Mintwood Place, N.W., Washington, DC 20009; (202) 667-6369, Fax (202) 319-1262; Rick Fenstemaker, gen'l mgr., Tamara Wood, host. Open all year. Thirty-one rooms, some with private baths. Rates: $40 to $95, with full continental breakfast and afternoon sherry. There are no provisions for small children; no pets; no personal checks; major credit cards accepted; limited smoking. Limited parking space may be reserved in advance for $7 per night. Over 50 ethnic restaurants to choose from in a 2 block radius.

DIRECTIONS: from Baltimore south on I-95, take the beltway 495 west toward Silver Spring to exit 33. South on Connecticut Avenue towards Chevy Chase. Pass the zoo entrance in the 3000 block and count 4 stop lights and turn left on Calvert St. Go to 2nd stop light and turn right on Columbia; 2 blocks down turn right on Mintwood.

MORRISON-CLARK

The Capitol's Historic Inn

Once two separate townhouses, this historic site evolved into the Soldiers, Sailors, Marines and Airmen's Club to provide affordable hotel accommodations for servicemen during World War II. First Ladies Mamie Eisenhower and later Jackie Kennedy volunteered time here to help with fundraising for the club's operations.

Morrison-Clark (the names of the two original owners) came into existence in 1987, when renovations were completed under the watchful eye of William Adair, who had supervised renovations at the White House. He made certain distinctive features were preserved: the Chinese Chippendale porch, the Shanghai roof, four original pier mirrors, and the Italian Carrera marble fireplaces, among other things.

Each of the 54 guest rooms is unique, many showcasing historical details. Original artwork and authentic period furnishings are complemented by custom designed hand-crafted pieces. Many of the rooms have bay windows, some have porches. An

Left. The wonderful old building that has been transformed into a sleek small hotel.

A carved marble fireplace.

expanded Continental breakfast is served in the Club Room, the original dining room of the Clark House—elegant with its carved marble fireplaces, gilded mirrors and custom designed bar.

You do not have to leave the inn for what Zagat touts is "some of the best contemporary dining in D.C." There is a choice of dining venues here: The Garden Room for gracious dining with its huge floral centerpiece; The Dining Room, an elegant Victorian drawing room, decorated with Chinoiserie; the Courtyard with a fountain and perennial plantings; or the Veranda, the grand front porch.

Morrison-Clark is the sole historic inn in the nation's capitol, and is much appreciated by its guests. One sent this thank you note:

"Everything has been five star. This is a charmingly elegant inn. Thanks for a memorable experience in Washington, D.C."

MORRISON-CLARK, Massachusetts Avenue and Eleventh Street, NW, Washington, DC 20001; (800) 332-7898, (202) 898-1200, FAX (202) 289-8576; Michael Rawson, general manager. Open all year. 54 rooms and suites with private baths. Rates: *weekdays*, $115 to $165 single, $135 to $185 double; *weekends*, $79 to $135 per room; includes continental breakfast. Children welcome; no pets; smoking and non-smoking rooms, no smoking in dining room; all major credit cards. *Guest services include:* exercise room on premises, complimentary newspapers, concierge, valet parking on premises, babysitting, laundry and dry cleaning, complimentary shoe shine, movie rentals. *Business and conference services:* facsimiles and photocopying, secretarial and clerical, notary public.

DIRECTIONS: in the White House area on Massachusetts Avenue, a main thoroughfare.

A luxurious guest room.

A Washington row house just 8 blocks from the capitol.

Innkeeper Helène Price slices freshly baked bread.

CAPITOL HILL INDEPENDENCE HOUSE

Centrally located

Imagine waking in the morning only ten blocks from the U.S. Capitol, within a short walk of the Washington Mall and the artistic, historic, and scientific cornucopia of the Smithsonian's magnificent free museums. That's the happy lot of guests of the Capitol Hill Independence House.

This three-story bayfront was built in the early 1900s. While this bed and breakfast may resemble its adjoining neighboring houses built at the same time, the complete restoration by the present owners has transformed the inside into a sparkling urban retreat. The host Helène is from France and has trotted the world with her husband Larry, a military lawyer.

Helène loves to show guests the parlor with a working gas fireplace, the large library where everyone is free to browse among hundreds of books, the Yellow Room, with skylight and its original claw foot bathtub, and the Rosemary Room, decorated in English country style.

It's hard to imagine a more convenient place to stay, almost at the very center of government and business in Washington, D.C.—and in the warm care of a young couple who want their guests to enjoy their home and one of the world's most fascinating cities.

CAPITOL HILL INDEPENDENCE HOUSE. Completely restored house close to most of Washington's major attractions. Two guest rooms with private baths and king beds. Owners/hosts Larry and Helène Price. Open all year. Rates: $100 single or double, including a continental breakfast with homemade bread and pastries. No children, pets, or smoking; English and French spoken; all major credit cards. *Represented by Bed & Breakfast Accommodations, Ltd. of Washington, D.C.; (202) 328-3510.*

DIRECTIONS: given when making reservations.

The parlor.

Some of the art nouveau collection.

LOGAN CIRCLE

Extravagantly restored

Extensively restored by two loving owners, this one-hundred-year-old Victorian mansion features original wood paneling, stained-glass niches, ornate chandeliers, and a Victorian-style lattice porch and gardens. A mecca for lovers of "Art Nouveau," its walls are covered with highly selective and artfully framed posters, prints, magazine covers, and advertising art. The hostess, a tireless collector, is constantly adding new pieces to her collection.

In addition to the house's own beautiful appointments, the owners have incorporated some Victorian gems rescued by architectural salvagers: gilded mirrors, intricately carved mantels, and glistening English tiles. Floral patterns combine with silks, violet walls, wainscoting, draperies, oriental rugs, Eastlake furniture, and vintage floors, creating a romantic ambiance. One of two parlors houses a working player piano with silk-fringed turquoise shawl.

Each of the five guest rooms is singular and charming. An additional ground floor apartment offers complete privacy and comfort. Guest room furnishings include antique quilts, wicker, greenery, shutters, wash bowls, a Jacobean desk, and a four-poster bed.

Overlooking a fountain and rose arbor, the latticed porch seduces with a promise to banish worldly cares. Here one can effortlessly return to the romance and elegance of by-gone days.

LOGAN CIRCLE. Six guest rooms with shared baths and 1 apartment with private bath. Open all year. Rates: $60 to $65 single, $70 to $75 double; apartment $65 single, $80 double; continental breakfast included. Children welcome; no pets; no smoking. *Represented by Bed & Breakfast Accommodations Ltd.*, P.O. Box 12011, Washington, DC 20005; (202) 328-3510, FAX (202) 332-3885; Visa/MasterCard/American Express/Diners.

DIRECTIONS: given on reservation.

Alexora at the breakfast table.

Innkeeper Alexora Skvirsky.

THE DUPONT AT THE CIRCLE

Where the Americas meet

At first glance the Victorian interior of the 1885 townhouse looks like a picture spread from *House Beautiful* or *Architectural Digest* of a contemporary North American home. But on closer examination, the guest sees many traces from both the North and South Americas.

The gentle force behind this fascinating combination is the hostess, Alexora, a native of Ecuador. Ecuadorian paintings and dolls, and art objects of South American ancestry accent many of the high-ceilinged rooms. The house has six working fireplaces with original mantels. Alexora's husband is a management consultant responsible for many of the home's practical touches, such as private phones in the rooms, a Jacuzzi tub, and beautiful bathrooms filled with virtually every amenity.

Located right in the heart of Dupont Circle, this two-country bed and breakfast blends in seamlessly with Washington's cosmopolitan lifestyle. It is also very convenient for business and pleasure travelers because they are only a block from the metro subway and in the midst of many of Washington's best restaurants.

THE DUPONT AT THE CIRCLE. A Victorian townhouse in the heart of Washington, DC; Alan and Alexora Skvirsky, owners. Open all year. Two bedrooms with working fireplaces, one with a 1900's sleigh bed. Rates: $90 to $190 single, $10 more double, including continental breakfast. No children; pets, or smoking; English and Spanish spoken (the hostess teaches Spanish at a local high school); all major credit cards. *Represented by Bed & Breakfast Accommodations, Ltd. of Washington, D.C., (202) 328-3510.*

DIRECTIONS: given when making reservations.

The other guest room's sitting area.

The Library guest room.

BED & BREAKFAST RESERVATION AGENCIES

District of Columbia

THE BED & BREAKFAST LEAGUE / SWEET DREAMS & TOAST, P.O. Box 9490, Washington, DC 20016; (202) 363-7767; Millie Groobey. 9 A.M. to 5 P.M. Monday to Thursday, 9 A.M. to 1 P.M. Friday. *Washington, D.C. and adjacent suburbs.*

BED 'N' BREAKFAST LTD. OF WASHINGTON, D.C., P.O. Box 12011, Washington, DC 20005; (202) 328-3510, Fax (202) 332-3885; Jackie Reed. 10 A.M. to 5 P.M. weekdays, 10 A.M. to 1 P.M. Saturday. *Washington metropolitan areas, specializing in the historic districts.*

Maryland

AMANDA'S BED & BREAKFAST RESERVATION SERVICE, 1428 Park Avenue, Baltimore, MD 21217; (800) 899-7533, (410) 225-0001, Fax (410) 728-8957; Betsy Grater. 9 A.M. to 5 P.M. weekdays. *Private homes, yachts and small inns in Baltimore, Maryland, and nearby states.*

THE TRAVELLER IN MARYLAND, P.O. Box 2277, Annapolis, MD 21404; (800) 736-4667, (410) 269-6232, Fax (410) 263-4841; Greg Page. 9 A.M. to 5 P.M. Monday to Friday. *Yachts, inns, private homes.*

New Jersey

BED & BREAKFAST ADVENTURES, Suite 132, 2310 Central Avenue, North Wildwood, NJ 08260; (609) 522-4000, Fax (609) 522-6125, (800) 992-2632; Paul and Diane DiFilippo. Vacation homes, refurbished mansions, apartments. *New Jersey, including seashore and Delaware River area, northeast Pennsylvania, and New York.*

AMANDA'S BED & BREAKFAST RESERVATION SERVICE, 21 South Woodland Avenue, East Brunswick, NJ 08816; (908) 249-4944, Fax (908) 246-1961; Orie Barr. Monday to Friday 8:30 A.M. to 5:30 P.M., Saturday 8:30 A.M. to 12:30 P.M. *All of New Jersey and Pennsylvania up and down the Delaware River.*

New York

THE AMERICAN COUNTRY COLLECTION, 984 Gloucester Place, Schenectady, NY 12309; (518) 370-4948; Beverly Walsh. *Northeastern New York. Vermont, Western Massachusetts.*

A REASONABLE ALTERNATIVE, INC., 117 Spring Street, Port Jefferson, NY 11777; (516) 928-4034; Kathleen Dexter. *Long Island, Nassau and Suffolk Counties.*

AT HOME IN NEW YORK. P.O. Box 407, New York, NY 10185; (800) 692-4262, (212) 956-3125, Fax (212) 247-3294; Lois Rooks. 9:30 A.M. to 5:30 P.M. Monday to Friday, 9:30 A.M to noon Saturday and Sunday. *From artists' lofts to brownstones to high rise accommodations. Hosted B&Bs and self-catering apartments.*

BED & BREAKFAST ASSOCIATION OF WESTCHESTER, P.O. Box 1134, Scarsdale, NY 10583-9134; (800) 255-7213; *Represents 9 bed and breakfasts in Westchester.*

CITY LIGHTS BED & BREAKFAST LTD., P.O. Box 20355, Cherokee Station, New York, NY 10021; (212) 737-7049, Fax (212) 535-2755; Yedida Nielson. 9 A.M. to 5 P.M. Monday to Friday; 9 A.M. to 12 noon Saturday. Two night minimum stay. *Hosted and unhosted apartments from studios to four bedrooms in apartment houses and brownstones in Manhattan, Park Slope, Brooklyn Heights, and Queens. Ask about Europe.*

NEW WORLD BED AND BREAKFAST, 150 Fifth Avenue, Suite 711, New York, NY 10011; (800) 443-3800; (212) 675-5600; Kathleen Kruger. 9 A.M. to 5 P.M. Monday to Friday. Two night minimum stay. *Hosted and unhosted apartments in high rises and brownstones in Manhattan.*

URBAN VENTURES, INC., P.O. Box 426, New York, NY 10024; (212) 594-5650, Fax (212) 947-9320; 9 A.M. to 5 P.M. Monday to Friday. Mary McAulay. *Manhattan and other boroughs.*

Pennsylvania

ASSOCATION OF BED & BREAKFASTS, P.O. Box 562, Valley Forge, PA 19481-0562; (800) 344-0123, (610) 783-7838. Fax (610) 783-7783; Carolyn J. Williams. Town, country, historic, and ski locations, city and country inns. *Philadelphia, Brandywine Valley, Valley Forge, Lancaster, Bucks County, and Mainline Philadelphia.*

BED & BREAKFAST CENTER CITY, 1804 Pine Street, Philadelphia, PA 19103; (800) 354-8401, (215) 735-1137; Bill Buchanan. 9 A.M. to 9 P.M. seven days. *Represents 50 places from simple to luxurious townhouses in Philadelphia's Center City, Rittenhouse Square, Antique Row, Society Hill, University City, Art Museum area.*

BED & BREAKFAST CONNECTIONS, P.O. Box 21, Devon, PA 19333; (800) 448-3619, (610) 687-3565, Fax (610) 995-9524; Mary Alice Hamilton and Peggy Gregg, 9 A.M. to 7 P.M. Monday to Friday, 9 A.M. to 5 P.M. Saturday. *Everything from historic townhouses to small, charming B&B inns.*

BED & BREAKFAST OF SOUTHEAST PENNSYLVANIA, 146 W. Philadelphia Ave., Boyertown, PA 19512; (610) 367-4688; Patricia Fedor. Old farmhouses, town and suburban houses. *Reading and Allentown area, Bethlehem, and Lancaster county.*

HERSHEY BED & BREAKFAST RESERVATION SERVICE, P.O. Box 208, Hershey, Pa 17033; (717) 533-2928; Renee Deutel. Call from 10 A.M. to 3 P.M. *Lebanon and Hershey, Lancaster, Gettysburg, Harrisburg.*

REST & REPAST BED & BREAKFAST RESERVATIONS, P.O. Box 126, Pine Grove Mills, PA 16868; (814) 238-1484, Fax (814) 234-9890; Linda Feltman. 8:30 A.M. to 3:30 P.M. weekdays. Farms, National Historic Register homes, apartments. *Main Penn State campus vicinity plus Huntington and Altoona areas and all of central Pennsylvania.*

Virginia

BLUE RIDGE BED & BREAKFAST, Route 2, Rocks and Rills Farm, Box 3895, Berryville, VA 22611; (800) 296-1246; (540) 955-1246, Fax (540) 955-1246, Rita Z. Duncan. 10:00 A.M. to 2:00 P.M. Monday to Friday; 9:00 A.M. to 12 noon on Saturday. *East and west of the Blue Ridge Mountains and the Shenandoah Valley, Virginia and West Virginia, Pennsylvania and Maryland.* Houses on the Histroic Register, mountain retreats, and traditional private homes within fifty to two hundred miles of the capitol.

GUESTHOUSES, BED & BREAKFAST RESERVATION SERVICE, P.O. Box 5737, Charlottesville, VA 22905; (804) 979-7264, Fax (804) 293-7791; Mrs. Mary Hill Caperton. 12:00 noon to 5:00 P.M. Monday to Friday. *"Jefferson Country" including Charlottesville and surrounding Albemarle County.* Anything from guest rooms in elegant estate homes to charming guest cottages.

BENSONHOUSE, 2036 Monument Avenue, Richmond, VA 23220; (804) 353-6900; Lyn Benson. 11:00 A.M. to 5:00 P.M. Monday to Friday. *Richmond, Fredericksburg, Williamsburg, and Petersburg.* Forty-five private homes and small inns with accent on historic properties.

BED & BREAKFAST OF TIDEWATER VIRGINIA, P.O. Box 6226, Norfolk, VA 23508; (804) 627-1983; Betty Furr and Ridgely Nash. 8:00 A.M. to 8:00 P.M. Monday to Friday. *Norfolk, Portsmouth, Virginia Beach, the Eastern Shore, and the northern neck of Virginia.* Town houses, private homes, and unhosted furnished apartments near beach areas.